PAD
parties

PAD
parties

The Guide to Ultra-Entertaining

By Matt Maranian

Photographs by Jack Gould

Illustrations by Robert Field

CHRONICLE BOOKS

SAN FRANCISCO

Library of Congress Cataloging-in-Publication Data available.

ISBN: 0-8118-3785-8

Manufactured in China

Designed by Shawn Hazen

Distributed in Canada by Raincoast Books
9050 Shaughnessy Street
Vancouver, British Columbia V6P 6E5

10 9 8 7 6 5 4 3 2 1

Chronicle Books LLC
85 Second Street
San Francisco, California 94105

www.chroniclebooks.com

Greatest thanks to:

Alan Rapp, Matt Bialer, Shawn Hazen, Nina Wiener, Neil Wetenkamp, Sharilyn Hovind, and Carrie Bradley

I'm also greatly appreciative for the input, inspiration, and contributions from:

Greg Andrews of Alley Cat Antiques, Francesca Arroyo-Moyano, Holly Belluscio, Trishy Berberian, Jennifer Blair, Sue Boudreau, Stephan Briere, Cyndi Cain, Marty Dunlap, Marge Ekparian, Jenna Evans, Tracy and Vanessa Farrer, Don Favareau, Jude Fitzgerald, Holly Gillies, Jennifer Hart, Dondi Hearn, April Heaslip, Robert and Glenda Holmes, Noria Jablonski, Carol Katz, Tony Lovett, Ty McBride, Mark Melchior, Thirty 9 Main, Mom and Dad, Maliki Mouthwarr, Eliza Murphy, Maxine Nunes, Jake Palazzo, Patty Palazzo, Miémes Pierre, Kathryn Retzer, Jill Rosenthal, Dave Rountree, Michael Rudokas, V. Vale, Christopher Wainhouse, Dina and Earnest Wilson, and Myung-hae Yoon

For **Devil Doll,** the life of my party

Table of Contents

Launch Pad

Introduction

The Pad mindset is not specific to an era or a particular school or mode of design—it's a spirit of reinterpretation, reinvention, and personal cultivation infused with a DIY fervor and an idiosyncratic vision. For many, this mindset is more than a way to embellish the place in which they live, it's a way of life.

My previous book, *Pad*, was designed to inspire and celebrate those who experience their home as a multimedia work-in-progress. It demonstrated to its readers that beauty, comfort, taste, and elegance are concepts wide open to personal interpretation and reinvention. The reason that *Pad Parties* seemed like such an obvious next step is that one of the greatest pleasures to be had in creating such a space is to share that space with others—and what better way to do that than with a great party?

So exactly what is a Pad party? Much like a great pad, it's an event that engages the senses and galvanizes the spirit. It's an experience you can't ignore. It's an occasion when your talents for bringing people together and styling a space work collectively to heighten the impact of each. A Pad party is the apogee of the Pad mindset, a separate reality, an occasion as individual as the person who created it.

This book is not a connect-the-dots for the clueless host. The ideas suggested in these pages are simply intended to inspire you to take your parties in directions they may not ordinarily go, and to help you get them there. Seemingly obvious but often overlooked aspects of party throwing are addressed here, too, because, when it comes to entertaining, it's the fine details that are so crucial to the big picture.

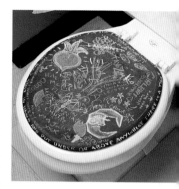

Pad Parties addresses basics like hors d'oeuvres and libations—but without ever making assumptions about the aptitude of the host in question. When it comes to matters of mixology, you'll find ways to hydrate guests with flair without spending the first hour and a half of the party with your nose in a bartending manual. And food, like drinks, need not be a daunting prospect for the neophyte or noncooking host. *Pad Parties* recipes have been selected and designed so that they can be mastered by those who consider themselves a culinary liability.

A Pad party is about much more than food and drink, though, so ideas for enhancing your partyscape with music and ambient oddities are featured as well; *Pad Parties* will provide you not only with a mix to fill your punch cup, but also with a how-to for a swanky table on which to set your glass. To help fill in the blanks, the source guide at the end of the book, "Note Pad," will direct you to product information, retailers, and suppliers for those items flagged with a "📓" that are featured in projects and sidebars throughout the book.

Perhaps most importantly, *Pad Parties* addresses the great balancing act you must perform as host: successfully managing your party without feeling like a caterer. The entire reason for throwing a party in the first place is to have a smashing time, and if clearing empty trays, filling ice buckets, and wiping spills are the only lingering memories you have of the night, you've done something wrong. *Pad Parties* will help steer you in the right direction so that you can both enjoy your role as host and the scene you've worked so hard to cultivate, because, ideally, a Pad party is an event that should be as much fun to throw as it is to attend.

Quaff

A Pad party is a place to imbibe in high style. Whether you're setting out a punch bowl or mixing to order, a drink is the first thing your guests will reach for when they walk through the door, and your bar—be it a swanky backlit built-in or an ephemeral tabletop grouping serving you only for the night—is the central nervous system of the event. But for the Padophile, the bar is more than simply a place to store bottles and stash glassware: It's an important embellishment to their partyscape, where swizzle sticks, power drills, lemon twists, and electrical tape all share equal time.

Limbo Bar Back

The timeless combination of the yellow from aged bamboo, the gold of lacquered rattan, and the punch given by a deep Chinese red is a cocktail lounge classic. It's evocative of greasy platters piled high with chop suey and glistening mounds of phosphorescent sweet 'n' sour pork, washed down with a syrupy cocktail garnished with paper umbrellas and maraschino cherries.

You can bring the tiniest taste of that tawdry spin on the Orient right into your own living room with this simple shelving unit. It provides an accessible spot for glassware or bottles of liquor and mixers when hung behind a bar or adjacent to the kitchen, and serves as an alternative for those without space for a freestanding bar. The dimensions of this unit—overall 37" x 36¾" x 8"—can be easily modified to fit a tight spot, provide deeper shelf space, or accommodate a greater number of shelves.

Tools

* Miter box with saw and cam pins (see Notes)
* Measuring tape or yardstick
* Fine-grade sandpaper
* Newspaper
* Electric drill
* $5/16$", $3/8$", and 1" drill bits
* Hammer
* Pliers
* Scissors or garden shears
* Hot-glue gun and glue sticks
* Level

Supplies

* 15' length of 1" diameter split rattan pole
* Spray shellac
* Three 7½" x 36" pieces of ¾" medium-density fiberboard (MDF) (see Notes)
* Paint (optional, see Notes)
* Wood glue
* 1 small box $5/8$" x 19 wire brads

* One 8' long, 3½" diameter bamboo pole (see Notes)
* Eight to sixteen ¼" cut washers
* Eight $5/16$" hex nuts
* Two 3' long, $5/16$" threaded rods
* One 4' x 3' sheet of rain cape thatch
* One 10" x 36" piece of ¼" masonite or luan board
* Two 3" corner braces and screws (see step 13)

Directions

1. Using the miter box, cut 9 pieces of split rattan at 45° angles to frame the face and sides of each shelf. Measuring from their longest points, you should have three 37" pieces and six 8" pieces, leaving the one end of each 8" piece (the end that will meet the wall when the unit is hung) with a straight cut. Sand away any rough edges. Working in a well-ventilated area, place the rattan pieces flat-side down over newspaper, and finish with two to three coats of spray shellac, allowing each coat to dry completely before applying the next.

2. At both ends of each piece of MDF, mark a spot 3" from the edge, centered. Drill a hole with the $5/16$" bit on each mark. If you're going to paint the shelves, now is the time. Let the paint dry completely before trimming with the rattan.

3. Run a thin line of wood glue along the front ¾" edge of the first shelf, and tack the split rattan trim in place with wire brads: place the first brad, centered, about 1½" from each cut end and space the remaining brads (you should only need a total of 5) evenly about 8" apart. When placing the rattan trim against the edge of the shelf, you may find that it doesn't provide a completely straight line, but it can easily be bent into place. Start by nailing the piece at each end, then push the middle of the rattan strip to meet the desired spot on the edge of the shelf. While holding the piece where you want it, secure it with a centered brad, and repeat if necessary. Next, add the side pieces of rattan trim, applying them just as you did the facing piece, using wood glue and wire brads. Complete the trim on the remaining shelves.

4. Cut the bamboo into two 12" sections, two 8^1/$_2$" sections, and two 14" sections. Avoid cutting directly into a node and cut one end of each 14" section to a 45° angle, with the lowest edge of the angle coming just above a node on the bamboo. There is enough bamboo to selectively cut so that you end up with nodes just below 45° cuts. Sand all the cut edges lightly to smooth any splintering. Set aside.

5. Using the 1" bit, drill through the center of the inner nodes of the remaining 4 sections. The threaded rod should be able to pass through the center of each bamboo section easily.

6. Drill centered holes through the inner nodes of the 14" sections using the ^{3}/$_8$" bit.

7. Place 1 washer and 1 hex nut at one end of each threaded rod. Slide the rods through the drilled holes from the underside of one shelf, so that the shelf sits on top of the washer and nut.

8. Slide one 12" bamboo section over each threaded rod, so that the bamboo sections sit on top of the shelf. Slide the second shelf down over the rods, followed by a washer and a hex nut, screwing each nut all the way down to the shelf but not tightening completely.

9. Before tightening the nuts, position the bamboo sandwiched between the shelves to be equally distanced from the edges of each shelf, and so that they are set back an equal distance from the front edges of the shelves. Since the surface of bamboo is irregular, apply these general measurements for the positioning of each post: 2" from the front edges of the shelves, and 1^1/$_2$" from the side edges. Once the sections are positioned properly, use the pliers to tighten the nuts screwed down to the shelf above, securing the bamboo in place. Repeat with the third shelf and the 8^1/$_2$" bamboo sections. Set aside. ▶

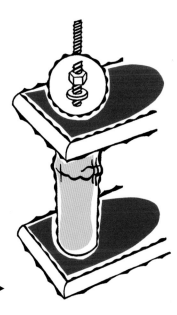

10. From the braided edge of the thatch, trim a section to measure approximately 40" wide and 18" long. When trimming the thatch, snip the webbing on its underside rather than making straight cuts across the layered topside. Secure the thatch with hot glue to the Masonite, folding and gluing the trim of the side edges to the underside of the board.

11. Slide the two 14" pieces of bamboo onto the threaded rods showing at the top of the shelf assembly. Work a washer over each rod, down to the node but not tightening completely, followed with a hex nut.

12. Place the shelving unit on its back, and place the thatched "roof" on top of the 45° angled bamboo sections, with the top edge of the roof board touching the floor. Using the board as a guide, adjust the bamboo pieces so that the angles are flush to the board. Tighten the bamboo in place, center the roof board and glue into place.

13. To hang the unit, screw two corner braces into the back side of the top shelf, so that one edge of the corner brace cradles the underside of the shelf and one side stands flush against the wall. Space the braces so that

they sit about 5" from each side of the unit. Secure the braces to the wall with screws, nylon sleeves, or toggle bolts appropriate to the wall, driving into studs if at all possible. Securing the unit to the wall is best done with the help of another person. After the corner braces are fastened to the shelf, hold the unit up to the wall, using the level to get the shelving straight, and mark the screw holes in the corner braces on the wall with a pencil. Remove the unit and drill leads for the screws. Reposition the unit and secure the corner braces to the wall with screws.

Notes:

A clamping miter box allows you to cleanly cut wood and other materials at 90°, 45°, and $22^1/_2$° angles. Miter boxes made of plastic are very inexpensive and well worth the purchase for building simple projects at home. If you've ever tried to cut an angle with a saw freehanded, a miter box will change your life.

Medium-density fiberboard (MDF) is sold in large hardware stores as shelving and in pieces cut to standard sizes. Two pieces of 15" x 36" MDF shelving cut in half will work best for this project. There isn't any reason you can't use another kind of wood for this job, but MDF is my preferred

material in that it takes sawing and drilling easily, doesn't splinter, has a smooth surface that doesn't require sanding, takes paint well, and won't sag or warp. And it's also very cheap.

If you plan on painting the shelves, use acrylic, water-based or oil-based latex, or spray paint. Any paint susceptible to scratches should be given one or two final coats of spray shellac.

When selecting bamboo poles, choose only those that are completely yellowed: any hints of green indicate that the bamboo has not completely dried, and those pieces are likely to shrink, split, or crack. Eye the poles carefully, choosing only the ones with the straightest lines. When cutting sections to use for this project, cut from the straightest sections of the pole, and count on several inches of scrap. Curved sections can't be used for projects requiring squared lines. Keep the bamboo stationary in a miter box with cam pins while cutting. Light, steady, and patient strokes from the saw will cut bamboo most effectively. Forcing the saw can cause a pole to shift or splinter. Sand in single strokes toward the cut end.

Sex Contact Cocktail Napkins

Do you know what a DOMBiPMJWF w/a great SOH is? I do, because I never miss the weekly adult personal ads. The personals are always the most compelling reading material to be had in those free arts-and-entertainment rags, and they beat any political editorial, horoscope, or crossword puzzle, hands down. The sex personal has its own distinctive syntax, ever evolving and developing into a new shorthand, and in doing so has produced a lexicon entirely unto itself. The grad school of adult ads, however, are the adult contact and swinger publications devoted entirely to such listings. The bonus here, should you care to see it that way, is that these ads run with photos; a wanton state-by-state exhibit of astonishing physical attributes, overeroticized self-delusion, close-ups fit for an anatomy textbook, and an inadvertent sampling of various surgical scars that haven't healed quite right.

From here we draw a straight line to that longtime party staple, the cocktail napkin. Since its inception, it has served as a medium for lewd limericks, suggestive cartoons, and adult jokes. This project simply takes the classic cocktail napkin into the twenty-first century.

Tools
* Computer, printer, and scanner
* Iron
* Scissors or paper cutter

Supplies
* One particularly explicit adult contact publication 📓
* 1 or more sheets of inkjet T-shirt transfer paper 📄
* Cotton fabric in a very light, solid color, cut into 5¹/₂" squares (see Note)

Directions
1. Peruse the magazine or newspaper for the images and ads that speak to you most. Bold, clear, high-contrast images scan best. Avoid mushy gray-toned images with a lot of detail. Clip the ads you'd like to use and scan them onto your computer.

2. Follow product instructions to print the scans onto the transfer paper.

3. Finish each fabric square by pulling off one thread at a time from along each edge, until you create a fringed edge about ¹/₄" long.

4. Position each transfer on a fabric square and iron according to product instructions.

Note:
One standard size of cocktail napkin is 5" square. You can cut the napkins larger to accommodate a particular image, but keep in mind that cocktail napkins are easier to handle if kept under 6" square. When cutting the fabric, make sure you're cutting square with the weave of the threads—otherwise you won't get an evenly fringed edge. Light-colored linen or plain white fabric will produce the best results, as the transfers are not opaque.

Stripped Down and Liquored Up

Pad Party Bar Basics

You can produce a wide variety of mixed drinks with a surprisingly modest assortment of ingredients. A well-provisioned Pad party bar doesn't need to include seventy-six varieties of arcane liqueurs, and only one good selection of each basic hard liquor is really all that's necessary. You can get carried away, of course—sometimes that's the entire point for the neurotic home-bartender—but if your aim is simply to offer guests a good selection of favorites, plus a few exotic alternatives, it won't cost you a month's salary (or more cubic inches than the bar shelving projects in this chapter provide) to stock your bar with the basics.

Although it's almost impossible to forecast, you can estimate the amount of alcohol you'll need for a party by assuming that every guest will consume on the average between two and three mixed drinks. Taking into consideration that each mixed drink includes about two ounces of hard liquor, that allows about twelve drinks per 750-ml bottle of booze. While you can assume the two-to-three-drink rule with hard alcohol, the same rule does not apply to wine. Expect wine drinkers to swill three to four glasses each, in six-ounce servings. This amounts to about four glasses per 750-ml bottle.

Many partygoers know their limit and after two or three hard drinks might want to taper off onto something a little less potent. That's why it's important to factor in additional quantities of sparkling and still mineral water, sodas, and tonic when writing up your bar list.

First, four staple hard liquors:

Gin

Gins can be divided between the harsh and the smooth, with a variation or two falling somewhere in between. Most gin drinkers love and expect its bite; others prefer a more amicable relationship to their cocktail, opting for a softer variety infused with a variety of botanicals. Although there is a range in quality, the "right" gin for the party bar is dependent entirely on personal taste.

Tequila

For tequila, there are two major distinctions: gold and silver. Between the two, you're better off stocking your bar with gold. It's generally a tequila of higher quality, and its superior taste makes it conducive both to shots and mixed drinks. Silver tequila serves almost exclusively as a mixer.

Vodka

Vodka is possibly the most popular of the hard liquors and a versatile component of a wide assortment of mixed drinks. Much like gin, vodka can be divided between the strong and the meek, but there are also distinctions among wheat, rye, corn, and potato vodkas. "Best" is ultimately a distillation of personal taste.

Whiskey

There is a multitude of distinctions within the world of whiskey, and it can be a dizzying path to travel. Scotch aside, whiskey ultimately—and serious whiskey connoisseurs will no doubt take issue with this generalization—boils down to two choices: straight as opposed to blended, the latter being sweeter on the nose and a whole lot cooler on the throat. The blends vary greatly, but Irish whiskey tends to please across the board and makes a safe choice for the party bar.

Next, a popular liqueur with versatility:

Cointreau

You're likely to get the most mileage from this cognac-based, orange-flavored liqueur; it's commonly used and easy to experiment with. Although most bartenders will use Grand Marnier (another cognac and orange liqueur) for some drinks and Cointreau for others (e.g., Grand Marnier for Margaritas, Cointreau for Cosmopolitans), you can use Cointreau interchangeably without incident.

Last, add these important particulars to the mix:

Club soda
Coke
Cranberry juice (look for pure juice without extra sugar or additives)
Ice
Lemons
Limes
Orange juice (freshly squeezed whenever possible—it will make a difference)
Rose's Lime Juice
Sweet-and-sour mix or **frozen limeade**
Tonic water

The preceding will be plenty for a party bar with a reasonable number of options. If you want to add extras, the next step on the pyramid of mixology could include:

Blue Curaçao

A liqueur made from the peels of sour green curaçao oranges, available in clear, blue, and orange variations. While there is no difference among the tints in terms of flavor, you'll be hard pressed to find a liqueur that adds more pow to a party than the curaçao of the blue variety; many guests will request a curaçao drink for no other reason.

Midori

A popular component of a variety of specialized drinks, Midori is a melon liqueur that pleases the eye, as well as the tongue, with a vibrant green hue.

Vermouth

For party purposes, vermouth will most likely serve only within the realm of the classic Martini. If you count any Martini purists among your guests, vermouth belongs at the top of your list, not the bottom. Generally, dry vermouth is the most popular choice among Martini drinkers.

Rum

Rum lends itself to a wide variety of exotic drinks, allowing you to incorporate coconut, lime, pineapple, and other quintessentially tropical additives.

Campari and Angostura Aromatic Bitters

If you're so inclined, these are perhaps the only bitters you will need, though you may find each bottle collecting dust on your shelf if you aren't an especially ambitious bartender.

Pineapple Juice
Though not as versatile a juice as orange and cranberry, it will add variety to your repertoire.

In terms of gear and gadgetry, your survival kit should include:

Shot Glass or Jigger-and-Pony Measure
These two devices serve the same purpose: to provide you with accurate 1- and 1½-ounce measures. Of the two, a line-measured shot glass is a little easier to master. If you're mixing a lot of drinks quickly without the advantage of a wet bar, the jigger-and-pony measure can end up making quite a mess. The handled, hourglass shaped, double-sided cupping of a jigger and pony measure have you inadvertently flipping liquer droplets and splashing expensive gin in places other than a cocktail glass, especially if you've knocked back a few yourself.

Bar Spoon
The most effective way to stir drinks is with a long-handled metal bar spoon. Generally speaking, a glass stirring rod is used to mix Martinis or anything carbonated.

Cocktail Shaker
There are a couple of varieties: one style (Boston) is more suited to function, and the other (standard) is more suited to flair. The Boston shaker is generally employed by professional bartenders and consists of a 16-ounce glass fitted with an opposing steel sleeve allowing for a tight seal. The standard shaker is what most would consider the "classic" shaker: a three-part contraption with a built-in strainer. They both get the job done. The choice is yours.

Cocktail Strainer
This tool is used in conjunction with a Boston shaker; you'll only need a strainer for drinks served straight up.

Paring Knife
Keep one of these small, sharp knives on hand for cutting wedges of lemon and lime. (Cut a good supply ahead of time.)

Combination Cork Screw/ Bottle Opener
Someone will undoubtedly bring a bottle of wine. Will you be able to open it? What about beer? Bottle caps are awfully hard on the teeth.

Ice Bucket and Tongs
The bigger the capacity of the bucket, the better. Ice melts. (Always get more than you think you'll need.)

Swizzle Sticks
These are especially important to have available if your guests are mixing their own drinks. Guests love swizzle sticks and often garnish their drink with one whether they need it or not.

Multitasking Cocktail Garnishes

An Hors d'Oeuvre Solution on a Stick

There are those cocktail party purists quick to harumph at the addition of anything more than a tiny twist of lemon, a thin wedge of lime, or a skewered olive in their drink, bitterly dismissing an artfully composed ten-inch garnish as superfluous excess. These are people who take life far too seriously.

On the other team, we have those for whom a garnish that stands nearly twice as tall as the highball glass itself is almost the entire point of a cocktail, rendering the actual drink secondary. For them, a cocktail is an event. These are the people who make good party guests.

A garnish for the sake of flash is fine, but a flashy garnish with a *purpose* is even better. Is it a drink? Is it an hors d'oeuvre? The answer would be yes. A cocktail that stands proud as a peacock but that also provides your guests with something to nibble on between swigs is what these assemblages are all about. And since the drink and the hors d'oeuvre is an all-inclusive assembly, they are left with one hand free to gesture, smoke, or write down a phone number on the back of a cocktail napkin.

Frozen Grape Swizzle with Flaming Lemon Rind

Serve with tropical, sweet, or tequila-based cocktails.

Ingredients
* Large seedless grapes
* 10" bamboo skewers
* 1 lemon, sliced into thin wedges
* Fresh mint sprigs
* Plain salad croutons
* Lemon extract

Directions
Stem the grapes. Bead 4 or 5 onto each skewer, sharp-end up, leaving $3/4$" of the skewer (the point) exposed at the top end of the swizzle. Place in the freezer on waxed paper until solid.

Slice the fruit away from a lemon wedge. Poke the bottom of the rind with the end of the skewer in a couple of places, slightly off center, and insert mint sprigs into the holes. Skewer the rind, centered, curled-side up, and push down to meet the top grape. Gently stab a crouton on the tip of the skewer, cradled in the lemon rind. Repeat with the remaining skewered grapes.

Use a teaspoon to soak the croutons with lemon extract, place the swizzles in drinks, and ignite the croutons just before serving. (These are best served when the grapes are right out of the freezer.)

The Enigmatic Wineglass

There are only two options a host has when caught short on glassware, and neither one is pretty: Option one, you'll have to waste valuable party time hastily collecting and washing whatever empty, lipstick-stained, or otherwise stray highballs you can scrape together in the moment and quickly recycle. Option two, you'll be forced to serve libations like Champagne, Martinis, and good red wine in juice glasses and teacups, which, for the host with any sense of pride, is reason enough to send everyone home right then and there.

To prevent these scenarios, learn to estimate ahead of time, but perhaps more importantly, understand the Enigma of the Wineglass. For the most part, you can expect guests swilling mixed drinks or punch to hang onto one glass throughout the night. However, this rule does not, mysteriously enough, apply to wine (or Champagne) glasses. For whatever reason, wine and Champagne glasses are twice as likely to be abandoned—after being emptied, of course—requiring a host to have nearly twice as many on hand. To avoid this, you can get little identifying rings that clip around the glass stems.

Sesame and Sweet Lime Grilled Shrimp

This garnish complements virtually any cocktail, as it is both sweet and tart.

Ingredients

* 1 lime, plus more for garnish
* 1/2 cup Rose's Lime Juice
* 1/4 cup rice wine vinegar
* 3 tablespoons toasted sesame oil
* 4 teaspoons kosher salt
* 1/4 teaspoon freshly ground black pepper
* 1 pound large raw shrimp, peeled, deveined, and tails removed
* 10" bamboo skewers
* Cilantro sprigs, for garnish (optional)

Directions

Slice the lime in half crosswise. Slice the bottom quarter (end piece) off each half and set aside. In a nonreactive bowl 🗑, grate the rind of the big lime pieces and squeeze the juice from them. Add all the remaining ingredients except the shrimp to the bowl. Stir well until the salt begins to dissolve. Add the shrimp and toss until completely coated. Cover and refrigerate for at least 1 hour.

Remove the shrimp from the marinade. In a grill pan over medium-high heat, grill the shrimp until lightly charred. With the sharp end up, skewer one of the lime ends, round-side down, pushing the lime about 4" down on the skewer. Interlock 2 shrimp and skewer them through their tails and bodies. Garnish with cilantro sprigs, if desired. Repeat to assemble the second skewer. Serve warm or at room temperature.

Blue Cheese–Stuffed Grape Tomatoes
with Sherried Onion Ring

Serve with drinks that lean to the dry side. The sherry brings out the natural sweetness of the onion.

Ingredients

* 1 large white or red onion
* Sherry cooking wine
* Ripe grape tomatoes
* Soft blue cheese
* Crushed walnuts (optional), toasted (see page 84)
* 10" bamboo skewers
* Fresh flat-leaf parsley sprigs, for garnish (optional)

Directions

Cut the onion into 1/4" thick crosswise slices. Place the slices in a deep bowl and pour in enough sherry to cover. Chill for 1 hour, covered.

Slice the top third off the tomatoes and, with the tip of a knife, scrape out the pulp and seeds. Using the tip of a butter knife, stuff each tomato with blue cheese, or a mixture of blue cheese and toasted walnuts, if desired. Chill until firm.

Drain the onion rings. To assemble, skewer the top side of an onion ring, then 2 or 3 tomatoes (whatever the diameter of the onion ring allows), then the bottom of the ring. Push to the top of the skewer. Garnish with parsley, if desired. Serve slightly chilled or at room temperature.

Parmesan Shell with Grilled Red Pepper and Basil

Pair these with high-octane drinks that might ordinarily take a cocktail onion or an olive.

Ingredients

* 1 red bell pepper
* Olive oil
* Kosher salt
* Freshly ground black pepper
* Large fresh basil leaves
* Grated Parmesan
* 10" bamboo skewers

Directions

Seed the bell pepper and slice lengthwise into pointed strips about ³/₄" at their widest end. Wipe a grill pan with olive oil and, over medium-high heat, grill both sides of the pepper strips until lightly charred. Remove the strips from the pan, place skin-side down on a plate or cutting board, and sprinkle with salt and pepper. Place a basil leaf on top of each grilled pepper slice, and roll into pinwheels. Set aside.

In a dry nonstick skillet over medium heat, sprinkle a thin layer of grated Parmesan in the size and shape of a large potato chip. Once the cheese begins to bubble and become lacy and slightly golden, gently peel up the edges with a spatula and loosen the center from the pan. Keeping the shape flat and circular, flip the chip over and cook the other side until just golden. Keep checking the progress to prevent overcooking. Remove from the heat, gently fold the soft chip over a red pepper pinwheel, and pin securely through the center with a bamboo skewer. (Practice making a few Parmesan chips—they're easy, but require some experience.) Repeat with the remaining Parmesan and pinwheels.

Serve within 45 minutes, at room temperature.

Consider the following for your own constructions:

* Carrot medallions, grilled or pickled
* Cheese, scooped with a melon baller
* Cocktail onions
* Edamame pods, boiled
* Ginger, pickled or candied
* Green olives, garlic or chili stuffed
* Kiwi slices
* Lemon, lime, and orange wedges or slices
* Maraschino cherries
* Melon balls, frozen
* Pepperoncini, stuffed with grated mozzarella or smoked gouda
* Pineapple wedges, grilled
* Red peppers, pickled
* Rumaki (page 56)
* Star fruit slices
* Watermelon rind, pickled

The Power of **Punch**

There isn't any reason that punch should be restricted to bridal showers, square dances, and bar mitzvahs. A good punch can knock your guests on their asses as effectively as any mixed drink. What's in it? Who cares! There's something harmlessly inviting about a punch bowl: one dip of the ladle, three dips, a half-dip refresher, who's counting? A punch bowl spells party, and it's an easy way to keep your guests lubricated without having to personally mix and pour two dozen drinks. It's a great way to round out wine and beer, and if some thought is given to the placement of the bowl, it can help prevent a guest pileup at the food table or bar.

Please note that the punch mixes offered here are not for the meek. Ideally, each recipe will serve twelve guests of moderate constitution. All are served iced. You can prevent punch from getting watered down by ice cubes (which melt too quickly) by providing an ice bucket and tongs adjacent to the bowl or by making an ice ring (how-to follows on page 28).

Pink Chihuahua

Use a good-quality tequila and your guests will swear that you laced this punch with PCP. Float with thin slices of lemon, orange, or star fruit.

* Two 750-ml bottles tequila
* One 350-ml bottle Triple Sec
* 12 ounces sweet-and-sour mixer or 1 can limeade concentrate
* 12 ounces fresh lime juice
* 6 ounces cranberry juice
* 6 ounces grenadine

Tending Bar

With a little information, even novice bartenders can mix drinks with confidence and flair. They can even successfully improvise and produce a reasonable facsimile of almost any drink by employing some general rules of thumb. These same rules and ratios will provide sound guidelines for adventurous mixologists looking to invent a libation of their own.

Hard alcohol: With the exception of purely alcoholic drinks like martinis and gimlets, generally only one-quarter to one-third of the total liquid quantity in a mixed drink is hard alcohol.

Fruit juice: When using juices like orange or cranberry, you can be generous. Three parts juice to one part alcohol, ordinarily. If you're incorporating two juices, combine them as you'd want to influence the drink, keeping the same three-to-one proportion. With lime or lemon juices, using more than half of the fruit in one drink is probably too much in most cases.

Sweet-and-sour mix: Use a mixer like this as you would fruit juice, or combine one part sweet-and-sour to one part fruit juice, or substitute a small amount of frozen (undiluted) limeade. ▶

Club soda: Use soda to give a drink some zip, using no more and (in some cases much less) than one part soda to one part fruit juice or other mixers. If soda is being used as an additive for a drink being mixed in a cocktail shaker, keep it from flattening by shaking the drink first, pouring, then adding the soda.

Liqueurs: These can easily overwhelm a drink if you aren't prudent with your measuresments. Usually just a splash will do the trick. If liqueur is being used as a major component to a drink—like an Orange Martini—one jigger (1½ ounces) would be the most to add. Liqueur can either be shaken into a drink to thoroughly infuse its flavor, or floated on top after the drink has been mixed.

Preparation: When stirred, alcohol will stay clean and eventually separate from the mixer. Shaking a drink vigorously with ice will blend the alcohol and give a drink a much smoother taste. When improvising, you may want to go shaken as opposed to stirred to help mask any mistakes.

Presentation: Don't ever underestimate the power of an attractive garnish and a classic cocktail glass. A well-presented drink always tastes better.

Levitation

A libation conducive to casual makeouts among near-perfect strangers. Garnish with a couple handfuls of fresh raspberries and float with thin slices of lemon or star fruit.

* 36 ounces raspberry vodka
* 18 ounces vanilla vodka
* 36 ounces 7-Up
* 9 ounces grenadine

The Pigkeeper's Daughter

Serve only in glasses with caramel-dipped rims (the caramel can be found in the produce section of the grocery store, usually tucked on a shelf under the apples). Float with thin slices of lemon and tart green apple, no seeds.

* 32 ounces vodka
* 48 ounces apple pucker
* 16 ounces freshly squeezed lemon juice

The Leilani

A posthumous tribute to the best neon sign Fresno, California, ever knew. Float with thin slices of lemon, orange, and lime.

* One 750-ml bottle lemon vodka
* One 750-ml bottle Cointreau
* 12 ounces Malibu rum (optional)
* 12 ounces freshly squeezed orange juice
* 12 ounces freshly squeezed lime juice or Rose's Lime Juice
* 12 ounces club soda

Snake Charmer

It creeps up on ya'. Garnish with shaved dark or milk chocolate (use a vegetable peeler).

* 30 ounces Kahlúa
* 30 ounces fresh-brewed coffee, cooled
* 12 ounces brandy
* 24 ounces half-and-half

Santa's Little Helper
(a.k.a. Dress over the Head)

No reason to wait till Christmas. Garnish with floating glaciers of vanilla or peppermint ice cream topped with crushed hard peppermint candy, or with chocolate-dipped peppermint straws serving as swizzle sticks.

* 24 ounces vodka
* 12 ounces peppermint schnapps
* 24 ounces club soda

Circus Freak

This punch is as sweet as pink popcorn and marshmallow peanuts, more fun than a contortionist. Garnish with thin orange slices.

* One 750-ml bottle vodka
* 12 ounces crème de banana
* 12 ounces peach schnapps
* 8 ounces freshly squeezed orange juice

(Not) Tending Bar

Personally, I'm always looking for ways to shirk my duties as host, particularly when it comes to tending bar. When I throw a party, I don't want to miss out on any of the action. It took several parties before I was able to develop what turned out to be an excellent method for effectively mixing drinks without sacrificing any of my personal party time.

I realized that almost everyone has a drink specialty. You'll find that at any given party, you've got a bunch of closet bartenders right under your nose, eager to mix drinks, thus alleviating much of the work otherwise shouldered by you, the host. I've got a few important guests that I won't throw a party without, and nearly every one of them has a signature libation. When a guest wants a drink with rum or a drink that's blue, I know just where to send them.

Bartending assignments have another advantage, they fuel the social scene. It is quite possibly the single most effective method for getting people to meet and interact during the first hour or so—during which you may experience more guest arrivals and drink requests than you can handle.

So if you're not up to tending bar, don't. Let your guests do it for you.

Sweet Lorraine

A tropical holiday in a cup. Garnish this with frozen cantaloupe and honeydew melon balls, along with thin orange slices.

* One 750-ml bottle vodka
* One 750-ml bottle Malibu rum
* 18 ounces Midori
* 30 ounces freshly squeezed orange juice

Glue Sniffer

High flying on a model airplane. Float with thin slices of lemon and starfruit.

* 13 ounces brandy
* 4 1/2 ounces rum
* One 750-mlbottle champagne
* 6 1/2 cups lemonade

Ice Rings

As long as you've got room in your freezer, making an ice ring is a cinch. No shortcuts, though: start the process at least two full days ahead because, depending on freezer settings, ice rings need a full 48 hours to solidify. What a disappointment it would be to release your carefully crafted ring from its mold just moments before thirsty guests arrive, only to find yourself with a broken icy shell dripping with cold water and lemon slices. Don't let this happen to you.

You can go with a straightforward approach, plain H_2O, no frills, or you can style the ring a dozen different ways with layers of citrus slices, decorative (nonpoisonous) foliage, herbs, and/or berries. Note: Do not use plastic figures or other nonedible items, as they can pose a choking hazard when the ice ring melts.

When you make an ice ring, use either an angel food cake or Bundt pan. If you're embedding items into the ice, work upside down (the bottom of the pan will be the top of your ice ring), in layers. Start by placing your first decorative layer in the bottom of the pan, then cover with one layer of either crushed or cracked ice (this will keep the fruit or leaves from floating to the top when you add water). Pour just enough cold water to cover the ice, and freeze. Once that first layer is solid, add another layer using the same method, embedding more decoration or not. Keep in mind that the ring does not have to made entirely of water. A ring of fruit juice, or using fruit juice for the cracked ice and water for the ring (or vice versa) can also produce interesting results. The cake pan need only be one-half to two-thirds full for a substantial ice ring.

Once the ice ring has frozen through, remove it by setting the pan into warm water for a few minutes until the mold loosens. Flip the pan, remove the ring, and place gently into the filled punch bowl.

Frozen Water Ballons

Another inventive method for keeping punch cold is the water balloon mold. Freezing water balloons will give you odd orbs and biomorphically shaped globules of frozen liquid, particularly if you use large rubber bands, strips of nylon stocking, or string to constrict the balloons into sections before you slip them into the freezer. Allow as much time to solidify as you would an ice ring, at least two full days.

Illuminated Punch Bowl

Get lit both literally and figuratively by making your punch bowl a beacon for thirsty guests. This simple illuminated base gives any punch a mysterious and alluring glow, casting mood light in a dark corner, adding a decadent edge to an outdoor bar in the evening, or simply providing a place for blotto partygoers to fix their gaze as slices of citrus spin and drift.

If you don't have a large, clear punch bowl and can't live without this particular scene-stealer for your next party, consider a rental company. Chances are you can rent the perfect bowl for less than the cost of the alcohol used to fill it. The rest of the materials can be found at any hardware store.

Tools

* Ruler
* Permanent felt marker
* Handsaw
* Electric drill
* $1/4$" and $3/8$" drill bits
* Medium-grade sandpaper
* Paintbrush
* String or clothespins

Supplies

* 8" diameter plastic painter's bucket (available at hardware stores)
* All-purpose glue
* Masking material for the exterior of the base, cut to a measurement of 5" x $27^1/_2$" (see Notes)
* Cloth tape, to match the exterior covering of the base
* Ceiling-mount light socket set (which should include 2 wire nuts and two $1/8$ IP hex locknuts)
* Two $1/8$ IP brass washers
* Lamp cord set with plug
* Electrical tape
* Two 40-watt (or less) appliance or chandelier bulbs
* Large, clear punch bowl

Directions

1. Measuring vertically from the bottom of the bucket, mark a point 5" from the bottom edge of the exterior. Continue to mark the 5" points around the circumference of the bucket exterior, spacing the marks about 4" apart (see Notes).

2. Using those marks as your guide, saw a straight line through the bucket.

3. Using the $1/4$" bit, drill a hole through the side of the bucket, about 1" from the bottom edge. This will provide a passage for the lamp cord. Using the $3/8$" bit, drill another hole in the bottom center of the bucket.

4. Sand the top edge of the bucket to smooth any roughness in the cut or to level an uneven line. Clean the bucket of all plastic shavings and dust.

5. Brush the exterior surface of the bucket with glue and wrap it with the masking material, placing the seam in line with the lamp cord hole. Use the string or clothespins to hold the material in place until the glue dries completely.

6. Mask the top and bottom edges of the bucket with cloth tape to finish the trim of the masking material. Run a line of tape vertically along the seam of the material.

7. Secure the socket set into the bottom hole of the bucket by first screwing a hex locknut onto the threaded stem at the base of the ▶

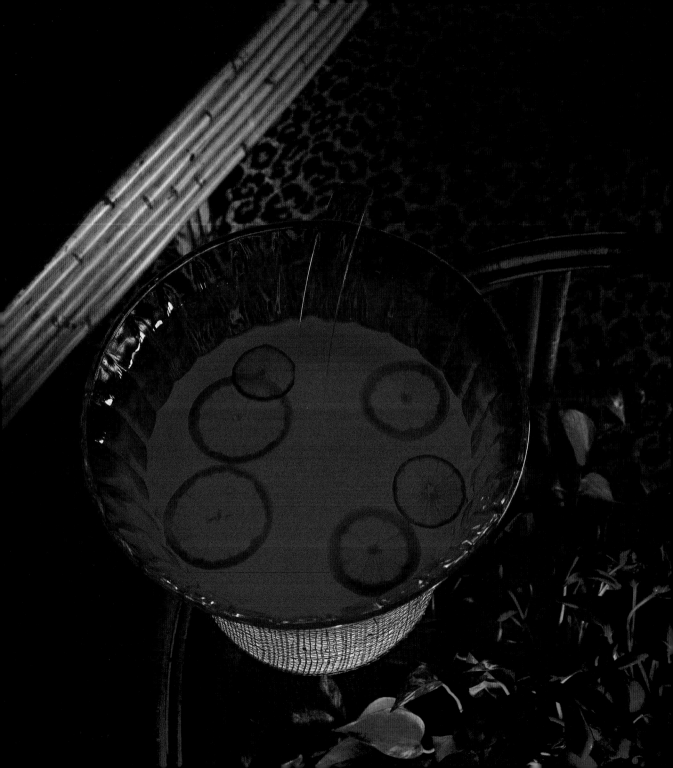

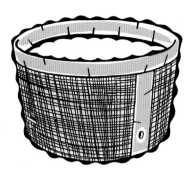

set, followed by a washer. Slip the stem through the center hole of the bucket and secure from the underside of the bucket with another washer and hex locknut. The bucket should sit flush on a tabletop without teetering.

8. Pull the exposed end of the lamp cord into the bucket through the exterior side of the lamp-cord hole. Attach the wires of the lamp cord set to the wires coming from the socket set: One end of the lamp cord set will be split in two with an exposed portion of copper wire at each of the two ends. One side of the cord will be ribbed, the other smooth. The wire coming from the *ribbed* side of the cord gets attached to the *black* socket set wire, the *smooth* to the *white*. Twist together the

wire connections, cover the end of the wire casing with electrical tape (leaving the joined wire exposed), and secure the connection by screwing a wire nut down over the top of the joined wire.

9. Screw the lightbulbs into the sockets. Coil the excess socket set cord inside the bucket around the elevated base of the socket set, making sure that the cord clears the bulbs completely. Secure the cord in place with electrical tape if necessary.

10. Center the punch bowl over the illuminated base, fill with high-octane punch, and dive in.

Notes:
You direct more light through the punch bowl by blocking the light

broadcast from the wall of the base. Mask the exterior with a material that allows a minimal amount of light to filter through. The material used to cover the base shown here is woven abaca matting 📕, similar to that used to make placemats and textured wall coverings.

Before cutting the bucket, consider the size of the punch bowl being mounted. You may require more clearance between the bottom of the bowl and the top of the socket set than the 5" base height suggested here allows.

Art Connoisseur Liquor Larder

Why wait for an artist to die before you get a return on your investment? An inferior art collection appreciates exponentially when modified to serve double duty as a handy booze cabinet, transforming a dime-a-dozen flea-market masterpiece into a bona fide one-of-a-kind.

Whether used in pairs or singly, any work in a wooden frame can be used for this project, as long as a set of hinges can be mounted on its backside. The very simple construction will provide the shelving and framework to support the cabinet doors, and embellishments like magnetic closures and doorknobs can be added to finish the assembly, or not.

Tools

* Ruler
* Saw
* Square
* Electric drill
* $9/64$" drill bit
* Medium-grade sandpaper
* Hammer
* Level

Supplies

* Artwork for cabinet doors
* 1' x 5' select $3/4$" pine planks (see Notes)
* Wood glue
* 12 or more 2" coarse-thread drywall screws
* Paint (optional)
* 1 or more $1/4$" luan panels, sized to the overall cabinet measurement
* 1" wire brads
* Cabinet hinges (1 set of 2 for each door), sized to the frame
* Magnetic cabinet catch (1 for each door) (optional)
* Cabinet knobs (1 for each door) (optional)

Directions

1. Set the measurements for your cabinet based on the size of the artwork you will use for the doors. Measure from the widest points of the flat surface on the back of the frame—this will be the overall measurement.

2. Using the pine planks, cut the four sides of the framework for the cabinet. The vertical sides should equal the full length you've determined. The top and bottom pieces should measure the full width of your determined measurement, minus $1^1/2$"; this will allow for the top and bottom pieces to fit inside the side pieces.

3. Smear the ends of the top and bottom pieces with wood glue, and assemble the cabinet framework by lying the pieces in place on the floor. Use the square to ensure right angles, and position stacks of large books, or chairs, to keep the pieces in place while the glue dries.

4. Once completely dry, drill leads (see Notes) for the screws at the top and bottom of each of the side pieces. The leads should be about $1/2$" from each corner. Follow with the screws. ▶

5. Cut one or more pieces of shelving equal to the measurements of the top and bottom pieces of the cabinet framework. Use the level to determine exact placement, skip the wood glue, and secure into place by drilling leads and using wood screws. Sand all the joined edges. If you're going to paint the cabinet, now is the time to do it.

6. Cut the luan panel to the overall measurement of the cabinet framework, minus about $1/4$" all around. Sand the edges, then, using the wire brads, attach the panel to the back of the framework. Space the nails about 4" or 5" apart along all 4 back edges of the cabinet and along the back edge of the shelves, to keep the luan panel from bowing.

7. Position the hinges about 4" from the top and bottom of the

frame. Fasten one side of each hinge to the back of the frame (the hinge pin should face the front of the cabinet door). It may not be necessary to drill leads for the hinge screws first; the screws that come packaged with cabinet hinges are small and usually fairly sharp, and should penetrate a wood frame easily without leads.

8. Lie the cabinet flat on the floor, luan panel–side down. With the hinges wide open, position the cabinet door in place. Fold the loose side of the hinge to lie flat against the side of the cabinet. Mark the spots for the screws. Remove the cabinet door and drill leads if necessary.

9. Reposition the door and fasten in place with the hinge screws. Last, add the magnetic catch(es) and cabinet knob(s), if desired.

Notes:
Pine is recommended for this project because it's inexpensive and easy to work with. Lumber is sold in different grades, "select" being the best cut. Select lumber will be free of knots, making the finishing process—should you want to paint the cabinet—much cleaner. Knots in the surface of the wood will never completely disappear, even when painted.

Drilling a lead is necessary before using wood screws because the pine will most certainly split, crack, or chip with the passage of a screw without a lead. The leads drilled should never be deeper than the screw is long. Generally, a lead about two-thirds the length of the screw will do the best job.

Ten **Hangover Cures**

It's the morning after, last night's party was a smashing success, and the only things keeping you from basking in its afterglow (which is the God-given right of every class-A host) are the brass band pounding between your temples and the nausea that you thought only expectant mothers experienced at this hour of the day.

If you're the type for whom an empty glass simply means another round or you've never quite mastered the fine art of moderation, you're probably the kind of lush that will try any hangover cure at least once. Should that be the case, here's a social season's worth of remedies for those inclined to overindulge. You're bound to hit on at least one that works for you.

Cure 1:
The Road Warrior

Is it truly possible to rock 'n' roll all night and party every day, day after day? According to a friend who's spent more time on a tour bus than he cares to recall, it is if you know the industry secret. It's a standby used by "hard-drinking rock band guys on the road" that falls under the Pharmaceutical Used in a Way Other Than That for Which It Was Intended category. In a word: Pedialyte. "It's used for infants with vomiting and diarrhea and replaces their electrolytes and minerals or whatever else you need if you're teetering on the edge of dehydration," he says, "and it's even sold in bubble gum and fruit flavors!" Just drink a glass before you retire for the evening—who ever thought a hangover remedy could taste so good? Wake up the next morning, jump back on the tour bus, hit the

next city, and do it all over again. And again, and again, and again, until you start looking like Keith Richards.

Cure 2:
Curl Up and Dye

This is an original tried-and-true remedy invented by my cousin-in-law Sue, a beautician by trade and a chemist at heart, and is almost as complicated as a triple-process bleach job. It's a combination of 1 ripe banana cut into small pieces, 8 ounces of water, and 4 teaspoons of liquid Mylanta, pureed in a blender and drunk, followed with ibuprofen (taken as directed). "This is a prehangover recipe," she insists, "meaning it should be done prior to passing out if at all possible!" How one might prepare the banana, handle the liquid measures of water and the Mylanta, operate a blender, and administer the correct ibuprofen dosage if you're drunk enough to need a hangover cure in the first place is almost as challenging as the nasty hangover that would otherwise follow, but this is just a testament to Sue's diligence. After all, she didn't become the owner of a successful salon by showing up to her beauty school exams bleary-eyed and barfy.

Cure 3:
No Stone Unturned

This method, of the cover-all-your-bases variety, was offered to me by a bartender pal. It includes both a prehangover measure and a morning-after scramble. First rule—if you're sober enough to remember this in the moment—is to stay up and awake an hour after you've stopped drinking. "Not really a cure," he admits, "but if you can just stay awake for an hour before you go to bed, you give your body a chance to break down the alcohol. Otherwise it just hangs around circulating through your system." The next morning—or afternoon, as the case may be—he advises a 30-minute hot shower and consumption of absorbent food (such as spaghetti, rice, bread, or potatoes), washed down with two "red beers" (equal amounts of beer and V8). Still not feeling up to snuff? "Morning sex and a few miles of running" should do the trick.

Cure 4:
Grease Is the Word

I was amazed to discover through my exhaustive research how many people use food to cure a hangover, with particular attention to the greasy variety. Foods saturated with grease, swimming in grease are the most popular: chili cheese fries, beef tacos dripping with lard, cheese enchiladas, biscuits soaked with bacon-fat gravy, jumbo beer-battered onion rings, fried chicken, bacon cheeseburgers, cuisine that settles in your stomach like adobe. According to many sworn testimonials, if you can hold this stuff down, it'll pick you right back up.

Cure 5:
Forbidden Fruit

My friend Rachel is awfully fond of tequila. Not margaritas, but tequila, straight. She asserts that the best way to avoid a hangover is to nix drinks mixed with fruit juices. "It's the sugar in the fruit juice that hits you hard," she claims, and insists that she can down straight shots of her favorite beverage all night long and wake up the next morning feeling refreshed. Not so with margaritas, she says. She also recommends B vitamins—maximum dosage—12 hours before, and suggests 4 ounces of aloe vera juice mixed with 4 ounces of water taken once in the morning and once in the afternoon, as a day-after stimulant.

Cure 6:
The Headbanger

What do Hershey, Pennsylvania, and Vergèze, France, have in common? According to my friend Dina, both of these towns produce important components of her personal hangover curative. She starts with three or four Advil washed down with Perrier, dismissing the dosage guidelines as a mere suggestion, and follows them with a giant Hershey bar. "The Hershey bar is for your pounding head," Dina advises, "although naysayers will tell you that chocolate is bad for a headache." The Perrier is for the nausea.

Cure 7:
Isabella's Revenge

A good pal and restaurateur modified this recipe, which she learned from her grandmother Isabella. Although it sounds more like a nice appetizer, which in fact it is, it serves double duty as a cure-all meal for the morning after. It has hair-of-the-dog properties, since it's made with alcohol, but those properties are only psychological since the alcohol burns off, reducing the risk of becoming a certified lush.

Combine ½ pound fresh shrimp, peeled, deveined, and tails removed, chopped; 1 cup chopped fresh fennel root; 1 cup diced roma tomatoes; and ½ cup Pernod in a large skillet. Sauté over medium-low heat until the mixture cooks down to a thick sauce. For a thicker sauce, sprinkle cornstarch, a half a teaspoon at a time, until desired thickness. For a thinner sauce, add chicken broth to taste. Accompany with toasted baguette slices, spread with anchovy paste, garlic, and olive oil, if desired.

Cure 8:
Pig Rinse

A native Frenchman, friend and hard drinker, shared hangover remedies from the region of France where he came of drinking age. Twelve raw oysters on the half shell with a light, cold, white wine is the common "brunch" for those nursing the nasty after-effects of a spirited night out. His second cure, which they call *rince-cochon* ("pig rinse" is a loose and somewhat poor translation), is a drink made from a 12-ounce beer, the juice of ½ lemon, a dash of sea salt, and 2 Alka Seltzers.

Cure 9:
Brain Storm

A friend who wishes to remain anonymous shares this authentic 1960s San Francisco hippie remedy. Formulated for those coming down from an all-night acid bender, it is said to work wonders for the common alcohol hangover as well. "If you can stand the taste," she advises, "just add 2 heaping table-spoons brewer's yeast to an 8-ounce glass

of orange juice and stir." Special bonus: A niacin rush is soon to follow, "but it only lasts a few minutes," she claims. Finally, chase the OJ with alternate hot and cold showers for as long as you can stand it.

Cure 10:
Desert Rose

Worcestershire sauce is to hangover cures what echinacea is to the common cold: It doesn't seem to serve any purpose or perform any real function, but people believe so deeply in its curative properties that a hangover remedy without it can seem strangely deficient. Desert Rose is a curious beverage made from 1 raw egg, 1 tablespoon Worcestershire sauce, and a shot of port, seasoned with freshly ground black pepper and celery salt. Drink this down while nibbling a dish of cold sliced cucumber sprinkled with kosher salt, and follow it with a double espresso.

Mastication 2

The recipe for good party food is a simple one: Avoid the predictable, plan ahead, and never attempt to serve anything so labor-intensive that it costs you any time away from your guests. If the trade-off for being able to enjoy your own party means piling serving platters with inventive room-temperature alternatives, so be it. A host's place should be within close proximity to their guests, not the broiler pan. With special attention given to party food of the prep-ahead variety, the Pad party recipes here provide an ambitious host with a reasonable plan of action, from nailing down the grocery list to passing the last hors d'oeuvres tray.

Hand to Mouth

Feeding your guests—it's one of the greatest challenges any host faces. How do you present something creative, appealing, and tasty without hiring a staff and taking a week off work to prepare it? Matters are further complicated if the most delicious thing ever produced in your kitchen has been microwave popcorn.

Proficiency requirements aside, when it comes to recipes, the most important aspects of party cuisine are often overlooked. For instance, can the item in question be prepped a day ahead without looking or tasting like it's been sitting in a refrigerator overnight? Can guests eat it while standing, and without using a fork? Is the time commitment required to follow the recipe reasonable? If you've grown beyond pigs in a blanket, and you're inclined to present something a little more interesting than hummus and crackers, the only thing standing between you and your desired results is a little planning—and the recipes that start on page 42.

While you'll want to provide your guests with something tasty and impressive, you won't want to spend the entire evening transferring things from the oven onto serving platters or keeping an eye on your watch to make sure you yank whatever you've got in the broiler before it catches fire. Personally, I like to experience the heights of carefree, sloppy, and otherwise good-natured inebriation right along with the rest of my guests, and I don't want to waste a whole lot of precious party time under the bright lights of the kitchen smearing whatnot onto hot crostini—especially if I'm unable to focus my eyes or steady my hand. Why should you be juggling white-hot baking sheets or inadvertantly scraping your knuckles across an unruly cheese grater while your guests are out there having all the fun? After all, a staggering percentage of household accidents occur in the kitchen and you don't want to be another sad statistic.

Herein lies one of the delicate balancing acts of entertaining: how to please your guests with an impressive spread of atypical edibles while enjoying free time playing host, rather than being reduced to a bumbling caterer who works for alcohol.

So maybe you don't know your way around Bánh Tráng. Maybe dolma sounds more to you like something you'd want removed by a good dermatologist than something you'd stuff with tabouli. Maybe you don't even know what the hell tabouli is. It's OK. Relax. There's still lots of room to surprise yourself. Even at the most fundamental level and employing a minimum of skill, party food can be duly impressive, well planned, stress free, and great fun to make if you don't pile too much expectation onto your plate.

Pad-Proven **Recipes**

The recipes collected here have come from many sources, and were chosen to offer a variety of influences from Asian, Mediterranean, Middle Eastern, and South American cuisines. The recipes are limited to ingredients that are best suited for serving chilled or at room temperature in order to make their preparation as enjoyable for the host as possible, with the least degree of performance anxiety. All of them have been party-tested as proven crowd pleasers, and all had to meet a stringent set of criteria in order to give hosts a sense of ease—as well as pride—and to provide guests with a savory, sumptuous, bite-sized feast.

Rule 1: Any food requiring a fork, spoon, or knife to eat is immediately disqualified. I like to make things easier on myself and my guests, so cocktail forks are about as close as I ever come to cutlery when I throw a party—if you've got to wrangle an hors d'oeuvres plate and a utensil, how do you hold a drink? The absence of cutlery also frees up some tabletop space, makes cleanup less involved, and eliminates the everyone-will-be-here-at-six-and-I'm-short-thirty-five-spoons dilemma. Besides, standing with a plate and a fork, trying to eat, drink, and carry on engaging repartee is awkward and smacks of a wedding reception. On the other hand, perching comfortably on the edge of a sofa with a highball glass and popping a tasty morsel from the end of an hors d'oeuvres spear into your mouth says Playboy Mansion.

Rule 2: Anything that has to be served immediately after it's prepared or pulled from the oven is no friend of mine. If you want to have fun at your own party, the food you serve should be able to sit and wait awhile—hours, some even days—before serving, so you aren't required to make a mad dash to the kitchen when you should be freshening your drink. Eliminating this kind of stress ahead of time is an important part of successful hosting.

Rule 3: No allowances are made for the obvious or the predictable. Guests want to be pleas-antly surprised when they bite into something, and crudités won't do it. Enough with cream cheese. And, for the record, almost no one likes anything that contains pimientos. Say no to tortilla chips and salsa (but say yes to Wonton Chips and Ginger Guacamole, page 85). There are tried-and-true standbys to consider, but a little reinvention doesn't do them any harm.

The recipes collected here were also chosen based on the degree of skill required to success-fully pull them off as well as on a sense of fun in their execution. You won't be required to use some kitchen gadget that you probably don't have, like a candy thermometer. It won't be necessary for you to fillet a whole fish, peel three pounds of grapes, or squeeze salmon mousse from a pastry bag. There is, however, one simple truth to party food: You can't wow anybody without putting forth a little effort. That said, if you've never worked with ingredi-ents like rice paper wrappers or if the broiler settings of your oven are as mystifying to you as quantum physics, no worries. These recipes are as suited for the culinarily impaired as they are for those with natural gastronomic flair; they're challenging enough so that you'll learn some-thing new, and they're tasty enough that you'll impress even yourself, never mind your guests.

Please consider that it never hurts to give a recipe a dry run before you actually serve it to guests. Practicing these once or twice, espe-cially when you're using ingredients you're unfamiliar with, will make you a whole lot more confident and improve your success rate. Feel free to improvise or embellish these to your own liking, too—if you want to use five cloves of garlic instead of two, substitute serrano peppers for jalapeño, or trade pistachios for walnuts, knock yourself out.

Recipes for **Meat and Seafood**

When you want to serve something substantial but haven't got the room or the wherewithal for a sit-down dinner party, these weighty hors d'oeuvres and abbreviated appetizers manage to sate appetites quite successfully, especially when rounded out with trough foods and copious amounts of alcohol.

Lobster Traps with Chili-and-Coconut Mayonnaise

This recipe makes great use of the wonton cup and is a tasty way to feed lobster to a room without having to take a cash advance on your credit card. The vermouth-soaked lobster meat topped with the chili-and-coconut mayo is an unexpected and flavorful twist on a crustacean most often served simply with melted butter and lemon juice.

Quantity: 16 lobster traps
Total Prep Time: 40 minutes
Head Start: The mayonnaise can be prepared a few days in advance if kept sealed and refrigerated. The wonton cups can be baked a day or two ahead and kept in an airtight container. The lobster can be prepped a few hours before serving and kept covered in the refrigerator.

Ingredients

* One 12-ounce package small wonton skins (3¹/₂" square)
* Extra-virgin olive oil
* 7 ounces precooked lobster meat
* 1¹/₂ tablespoons dry vermouth
* 1 tablespoon freshly squeezed lemon juice

Mayonnaise

* 1 small jalapeño pepper, stemmed, seeded, and minced
* 1 clove garlic, minced
* 2 tablespoons chopped fresh cilantro leaves
* 1 tablespoon freshly squeezed lime juice
* ¹/₄ cup canned unsweetened coconut milk
* 1 cup best-quality mayonnaise
* 3 firmly packed tablespoons shredded, dried coconut
* ¹/₄ teaspoon sugar
* ¹/₂ teaspoon kosher salt
* ¹/₈ teaspoon freshly ground black pepper

* 1 small bunch cilantro
* ²/₃ cup shredded, dried coconut
* Freshly ground black pepper

Directions

Preheat the oven to 350°F. Lightly brush both sides of each wonton skin with olive oil, and press 1 skin into each cup of a 12-cup mini-muffin pan. Bake for 8 to 10 minutes, watching to see that the corners of the skins don't burn. Remove from the pan and let cool.

Rinse the lobster pieces with cold water and pat dry with paper towels. Combine and toss with the vermouth and lemon juice in a small nonreactive bowl 📖. Chill, covered, until ready to serve.

Meanwhile, make the mayonnaise: Combine the jalapeño, garlic, chopped cilantro, lime juice, coconut milk, mayonnaise, and coconut in a food processor until blended. Add the sugar, salt, and pepper and process until smooth. Ideally, the mayonnaise should be refrigerated for an hour or two before using, to let the flavors blend.

To assemble, place a few sprigs of cilantro on the bottom of each wonton cup, allowing some of the leaves to rest over the edge. Place a heaping tablespoon or so of lobster meat over the cilantro, and top with a heaping teaspoon of chili-and-coconut mayo. Finish with a pinch of shredded coconut and ground black pepper.

Vietnamese Spring Rolls
with Sweet Chili Dipping Sauce

These cold rolls are standard at most Thai and Vietnamese restaurants, and always a hit with party guests. Although the ingredients seldom vary, the difference in quality and taste can be significant. If you're not crazy about shrimp, cold rice noodles can serve as a substitute, as the real flavor of the rolls lies in the basil, mint, and cucumber. The key is crispness and freshness, so always use the finest produce you can get your hands on.

Quantity: 16 rolls
Total Prep Time: 1 hour
Head Start: The rolls can be prepared a couple of hours before serving and kept covered, airtight, in the refrigerator. The sauce can be prepared early in the day and kept in the refrigerator, sealed in an airtight container.

Ingredients

* 1 cucumber
* 2 whole carrots, peeled (or 1 small package shredded carrots)
* 4 or 5 fresh shiitake mushrooms
* One 12-ounce package Bánh Tráng (rice paper wrappers; see Note)
* 1 bunch fresh basil leaves
* 1 bunch fresh mint leaves
* 5 ounces mung bean sprouts
* 1 pound large cooked shrimp, peeled, deveined, and tails removed, sliced in half down the center

Dipping sauce

* 1 red chili pepper, stem, seeds, and white membranes removed, minced
* 1 clove garlic, minced
* 1 teaspoon sugar
* 3 tablespoons water
* 1 tablespoon rice vinegar
* 3 tablespoons fish sauce

Directions

Peel the cucumber, slice it in half crosswise, and, with a vegetable peeler, shave it into 4-inch strips, avoiding portions with seeds. With the vegetable peeler, make strips from the carrots the same way. Wipe the mushroom caps with a damp towel (rather than rinsing to avoid water absorption), remove the stems, and slice caps into thin strips.

Fill a large pot (large enough so that the wrappers can lie flat and be completely submerged) with very warm water. Soak the rice paper 2 or 3 sheets at a time, for a few minutes, until soft and pliable (see Note). Remove from the water and place flat, in a single layer on a clean dish towel to dry, just long enough so they are no longer dripping wet, but still moist.

Place a prepared wrapper on a clean plate or work surface. Place 2 or 3 large leaves *each* of basil and mint in the center lower half of the wrapper, horizontally. The bed of leaves should ideally be about 4$\frac{1}{2}$-inches wide. Add a thin layer (2 or 3 pieces each) of cucumber and carrot shavings lengthwise over the leaves. Continue with a few bean sprouts, then a thin line of mushroom slices, and top with 3 or 4 pieces ▶

of sliced shrimp side by side in a single layer. Work closely so that these filling ingredients are tightly layered and form a neat, compact, rounded rectangle in the center of the wrapper.

To roll, first fold the left and right sides of the wrapper over the ends of the filling, creating 2 straight folded sides. Next bring the bottom half of the wrapper up and over the filling, doing your best to tuck its edge under the filling as firmly as possible. Holding the side folds in place, gently roll the wrapper tightly into a firm cylinder, then set on a serving plate, seam-side down. Repeat with the remaining wrappers and filling. If the rolls refuse to keep their shape, dab a little water under the edge of the wrapper to help seal it into place. Place on a serving tray, cover with plastic wrap, and refrigerate until ready to serve.

To make the dipping sauce, in a nonreactive bowl, combine all the ingredients and stir until the sugar has completely dissolved. Seal in an airtight container and refrigerate until ready to serve.

Note:
If you've never used rice paper wrappers before, experiment with them first. They are one of the most intriguing ingredients you'll ever use in the kitchen. They are actually quite forgiving, but require a little familiarity to use successfully. Play with several before you set out to make these rolls. Experiment with water temperature and soaking time. Soften the wrappers to achieve a variety in pliability; pull them, stretch them, fold them, and bite them to give yourself an idea of how soft they should feel, how long they should soak, and how hot you should keep the water. Experiencing these in a good Vietnamese or Thai restaurant will give you the best idea of the optimal consistency.

Kitchen Gear:
A Well-Appointed Arsenal

Use a steak knife to chop an onion or mix something with a fork instead of a whisk, and no one's going to be the wiser. A paintbrush, however—no matter how thoroughly it was washed after you finished the trim in your living room—should not be used to prep toasted baguettes with basil oil. There are tools for the cook that perform a specific job, and digging through the bottom of your kitchen drawers is probably not going to produce a viable alternative if you're caught without them.

When a recipe calls for a particular device, you should employ it if you expect adequate results. For the recipes featured here, there will be no surprises if you have this bare-bones arsenal of kitchen gadgetry on hand:

* Baking dish, covered and oven-proof, medium
* Baking sheet, preferably non-stick to avoid oiling ▶

Black Olive and Herb **Turkey Balls**

My wife, Loretta—an Italian with all due respect—calls these Guinea Meatballs, and they're an hors d'oeuvres spin on my own turkey meatloaf. Rather than formed in a loaf pan, the mixture is rolled into small balls, topped with ground pepper, baked, and served in a chafing dish to keep warm, with cocktail picks nearby.

Quantity: About 20 meatballs
Total Prep Time: 45 minutes
Head Start: The mixture can be prepared early in the day, covered, and refrigerated until ready to bake.

Ingredients

* 1 pound ground turkey breast meat
* $1/2$ red onion, finely chopped
* $3/4$ cup Italian seasoned bread crumbs
* 1 cup chopped mushrooms
* $1/2$ cup drained and chopped oil-packed sun-dried tomatoes
* 5 cloves garlic, minced
* 3 tablespoons chopped fresh basil leaves
* $1/2$ teaspoon finely chopped fresh rosemary leaves
* 1 tablespoon chopped fresh flat-leaf parsley leaves
* 3 tablespoons pitted and chopped oil-cured black olives
* $1/4$ teaspoon freshly ground black pepper
* $1/4$ cup olive oil (mix extra-virgin olive oil with the oil from the tomato jar to equal $1/4$ cup)

Directions

Preheat the oven to 400°F. Combine all the ingredients in a large bowl. Using a fork, or clean hands, mix well. Pinch off a bit of the mixture and roll it into a ball about 1-inch in diameter. Repeat to make about 20 meatballs. Place the meatballs on a lightly oiled baking sheet about 1-inch apart. Bake for 30 minutes, or until dark golden brown. Serve warm or at room temperature.

* Bamboo or wood skewers
* Bread knife
* Broiler pan
* Chef's chopping knife
* Food processor
* Grater
* Grill pan, nonstick
* Measuring cups for liquids and dry ingredients
* Melon baller, small
* Muffin pan, mini
* Nonreactive mixing bowls, small, medium, and large
* Pastry brush
* Pepper mill
* Potato masher
* Saucepan, medium
* Skillet, nonstick, large
* Slotted spoon
* Spatulas, metal and rubber
* Tablespoon and teaspoon measures
* Vegetable peeler
* Waxed paper
* Wire whisk
* Wooden spoon

Tequila and Lime Scallops

This dish is the best of all possible worlds: It's a guaranteed orgasm for seafood aficionados, it can be prepared hours ahead of time—the longer it sits in the refrigerator the better it tastes—and its presentation can't be beat. The toughest part of this recipe is finding enough half shells to serve a roomful of hungry guests, so start combing the beach in advance (see Note).

Quantity: 12 servings
Total Prep Time: 35 minutes
Head Start: The scallop and shallot mixture can be prepared earlier in the day and kept in an airtight container in the refrigerator. The cilantro and jicama mixture can be prepped and refrigerated early in the day as well, but should be kept separately prior to serving.

Ingredients

* 12 medium scallops (1¹/₂" or so in diameter)
* 4 teaspoons extra-virgin olive oil
* 4 tablespoons tequila
* ¹/₂ cup finely chopped shallots
* ¹/₂ teaspoon crushed red pepper flakes
* ¹/₂ cup white wine vinegar
* ¹/₂ cup lime juice
* ¹/₂ cup water
* ¹/₄ cup finely diced or 2" matchstick jicama
* ¹/₃ cup chopped cilantro leaves
* 12 clean scallop half shells (see Note)
* Kosher salt
* Freshly ground black pepper
* 12 small lime wedges

Directions

Rinse the scallops and pat dry with paper towels. Heat 3 teaspoons of the olive oil and 2 tablespoons of the tequila in a large skillet over medium-high heat. Just when the oil mixture begins to pop, add the scallops and cook 1 or 2 minutes on each side until they are opaque and seared. Remove from the skillet and set aside in a nonreactive bowl.

In a clean skillet, combine the remaining 1 teaspoon olive oil and 2 tablespoons tequila. Once hot, add the shallots and red pepper flakes and stir for 2 or 3 minutes. Add the vinegar, lime juice, and water and bring the mixture to a boil. Cook over medium-high heat until almost all the liquid has evaporated. Pour the mixture over the scallops, cover, and refrigerate until thoroughly chilled.

To serve, gently toss the jicama and cilantro with the scallop mixture and spoon 1 scallop along with 1 teaspoon or so of the salsa into a half shell. Top with a pinch of salt and black pepper and add a lime wedge. Serve with cocktail forks or picks, depending on the size of the scallops.

Note:
Scallop half shells can be found in craft stores and cookware shops.

Prosciutto and Basil-Wrapped Shrimp

This impressive broiled hors d'oeuvre is basically rumaki moved uptown (see page 56). Rarely in life do you really get what you pay for, but this is one salient example of a moderate investment yielding a high return.

Quantity: 20 servings
Total Prep Time: 35 minutes, plus 30 or more minutes for shrimp to marinate
Head Start: The shrimp can be marinated the night before, rolled early in the day, and refrigerated in a shallow dish covered in plastic wrap. Broil up to 1 hour ahead.

Ingredients

* 3 tablespoons white wine vinegar
* 3 tablespoons balsamic vinegar
* 2 tablespoons Dijon mustard
* 1½ tablespoons minced garlic
* 1 tablespoon sugar
* ¼ teaspoon freshly ground black pepper
* 1 cup extra-virgin olive or basil oil
* 20 large fresh shrimp, peeled and deveined, with tails intact
* ½ pound thinly sliced prosciutto
* 40 large, fresh basil leaves
* 20 wooden cocktail picks or bamboo skewers, soaked in water for 30 minutes (see Notes)

Directions

Combine the vinegars, mustard, garlic, sugar, pepper, and oil in a large nonreactive mixing bowl 📖 and whisk until thoroughly blended. Add the shrimp and toss, coating completely, then cover. Refrigerate for at least 30 minutes and up to 2 hours.

Preheat the broiler and position the rack 4 to 6 inches from the heat source. Trim the prosciutto slices to about 4 inches square. Place one slice flat on a work surface, then place 1 or 2 basil leaves along its lower edge. Place a shrimp lengthwise on top of the basil, with the tail extending over the side edge of the prosciutto so that it clears the roll completely (see Notes). Roll the basil leaf and shrimp tightly in the prosciutto slice and skewer diagonally with a pick or thread onto a bamboo skewer. Repeat to assemble the remaining shrimp, fitting three on a skewer.

Broil for about 15 minutes, turning every 5, or until the prosciutto is crisp and the shrimp has turned pink. Remove from the broiler and lightly brush with additional marinade. Remove from the skewers after the shrimp is cool enough to touch. Insert hors d'oeuvre spears for serving, if desired. Best if served within 30 minutes.

Notes:
Soaking the skewers in water prior to using them is important for the simple reason that they will catch fire during the broiling process if you don't.

To prevent the shrimp tails from getting singed, cover them with small pieces of aluminum foil before placing them in the broiler.

Larb in **Cabbage Leaf Bundles**

Cool and refreshing but packed with a punch, these larb (chopped meat salad from Southeast Asia) bites are the most pleasing way to pass off cold chicken to party guests. The cabbage leaves turn a vibrant green and make for a good presentation against a leafy bed of Italian parsley. The bundles also lend themselves well to decorative skewer action.

Quantity: About 12 bundles
Total Prep Time: 1 hour, plus additional time for the chicken mixture to cool
Head Start: The chicken mixture and cabbage leaves can be prepared early in the day and kept refrigerated. The bundles can be rolled an hour or two before serving and kept refrigerated.

Ingredients

* 2 heads green cabbage
* $1/3$ cup finely chopped green onion
* $1/4$ cup chopped cilantro leaves
* $1/4$ cup freshly squeezed lime juice
* 3 cloves garlic, minced
* 2 tablespoons minced fresh jalapeño peppers (stems, seeds, and white membranes removed)
* 2 tablespoons hoisin sauce
* One 14-ounce can chicken broth
* $1/2$ pound ground white chicken meat
* Kosher salt
* Hors d'oeuvres spears

Directions

Cut the stem end off each head of cabbage and carefully peel off 12 or more large leaves. Trim the thick ribs from each leaf, keeping the leaves as large as possible. Set aside.

Combine the green onion, cilantro, lime juice, garlic, jalapeños, and hoisin in a non-reactive bowl 📖 and set aside.

Bring the chicken broth to a boil in a large saucepan. Place the cabbage leaves 2 or 3 at a time into the broth and reduce the heat to a simmer. Cover and simmer until the leaves are soft-ened, 1 or 2 minutes. Using a slotted spoon, transfer the leaves to a bowl of cold water. Drain the leaves, pat dry, and set aside.

Discard all but $1/4$ cup of the broth in the saucepan. Add the ground chicken and stir over medium heat until the meat is cooked through (the ground chicken will clump up—break the clumps apart while cooking). Drain the chicken, add a pinch or two of salt, and toss into the hoisin mixture. Cover and refrigerate until cooled throughout.

Place a cabbage leaf flat on a work surface. Mound about 1 heaping tablespoon of the chicken mixture in the center of the leaf, fold over each side, and twist into a small bundle. Skewer closed with an hors d'oeuvres spear. Repeat with the remaining cabbage leaves and chicken.

Gutless Rumaki

Rumaki was the sour cream and powdered onion soup dip of its day, a cocktail party stand-by for so many years that it finally fell out of fashion. Traditional rumaki is made with chicken livers and bacon, but since folks don't gobble chicken livers the way they used to, they've been omitted from this recipe. However, there's no arguing with the taste buds of your guests when it comes to bacon. Anything with bacon is the first item to get wolfed down. When I throw a party, I like to personally pass the rumaki tray because the spectacle of my guests swarming like ducks at a petting zoo makes all the effort required to individually roll these cholesterol-packed bundles worthwhile.

Quantity: About 36 rumaki
Total Prep Time: 40 minutes, plus 30 minutes for the rumaki to marinate
Head Start: The bundles can be rolled, placed on a baking sheet, and covered up to 4 hours in the refrigerator before baking.

Ingredients

* 1/2 cup soy sauce
* 1 teaspoon minced fresh ginger
* 1/2 teaspoon curry powder (optional)
* 1/2 pound sliced bacon
* Two 8-ounce cans whole water chestnuts, drained
* Wooden toothpicks
* Brown sugar

Directions

Stir the soy sauce, ginger, and curry powder, if using, together in a measuring cup and set aside. Cut the scrappy quarter end off each bacon slice, making for a strip measuring about 6 inches long. Snugly roll each bacon slice over a water chestnut and skewer with a toothpick.

Place the rumaki in a single layer on the bottom of a shallow dish, then pour the soy sauce mixture over, carefully drenching each roll. Let sit, covered and refrigerated, for about 1 hour.

Preheat the broiler and position the rack 4 to 6 inches from the heat source. Spread a generous layer of brown sugar on a plate. Dredge each rumaki in the brown sugar, getting as good a coverage as possible. Place the rumaki 1 or 2 inches apart in a broiler pan and broil for about 10 minutes, turning frequently until the bacon is crisp.

The low road:

Avoid the broiler and all the hot grease runoff by substituting precooked vacuum-packed bacon for the raw stuff. On a baking sheet lightly coated with cooking spray, bake in a preheated 350°F oven for about 12 minutes, or until the bacon is very crisp without being burned. The difference in the finished product is minute.

Crab Cups with Roasted Red Pepper Sauce

Who can refuse a good crab cake? These lend themselves well to eating while standing since they're less like cakes and more like dollops, and are served in their own crunchy cups along with a tangy sauce.

Quantity: 30 crab cups
Total Prep Time: 1 hour and 20 minutes
Head Start: The wonton cups can be baked a day or two beforehand and kept in an airtight container. The red pepper sauce is actually better when made a day or two before and kept refrigerated in an airtight container. The crab mixture can be prepared up to 1 day before and kept refrigerated until ready to use.

Ingredients

Cups
* One 12-ounce package small wonton skins ($3\frac{1}{2}$" square)
* Sesame oil

Sauce
* 1 cup roasted red peppers, drained and chopped
* 2 tablespoons chopped fresh flat-leaf parsley
* 3 cloves garlic, minced
* 6 tablespoons best-quality mayonnaise
* 1 tablespoon Dijon mustard
* $\frac{1}{2}$ teaspoon freshly squeezed lemon juice
* $\frac{1}{8}$ teaspoon kosher salt
* $\frac{1}{8}$ teaspoon freshly ground black pepper

Crab "Cakes"
* 2 large egg whites
* 4 teaspoons Dijon mustard
* 3 tablespoons best-quality mayonnaise
* 1 tablespoon lemon juice
* Two 6-ounce cans fancy white crab meat, or 12 ounces cooked crab meat, drained
* 1 cup white bread crumbs
* $\frac{1}{4}$ cup finely chopped green onion
* 1 teaspoon grated lemon zest (see Note, page 77)
* 2 tablespoons chopped fresh flat-leaf parsley
* $\frac{1}{2}$ teaspoon kosher salt
* $\frac{1}{4}$ teaspoon cayenne pepper
* Butter
* Canola oil
* 1 small bunch watercress,

Directions

Preheat the oven to 350°F. Using several pans or working in batches, lightly brush both sides of each wonton skin with sesame oil, then press 1 skin into each cup of a mini-muffin pan. Bake for 8 to 10 minutes, watching to see that the corners of the skins don't burn. Remove from the pan and let cool.

Puree all the sauce ingredients in a food processor or blender until smooth. Cover and refrigerate until ready to serve.

Whisk the egg whites, mustard, mayonnaise, and lemon juice together in a large bowl. Add the crab, bread crumbs, green onion, lemon zest, parsley, salt, and cayenne and mix well. Form ▶

a crab "cake" by pressing a heaping mound into a lightly oiled teaspoon. Flatten and shape compactly, then transfer to a plate. Repeat with remaining crab mixture.

Melt 1 tablespoon butter with 1 tablespoon canola oil in a large skillet over medium-high heat. Cook the crab cakes in batches until golden brown, crisp, and cooked through, about 3 minutes on each side. Transfer to paper towels to drain. Add more butter and oil as necessary. If the butter begins to smoke between batches, wipe out the skillet with a damp sponge, let cool for a few minutes, and begin with fresh butter and oil.

To serve, place a few leaves of watercress inside each wonton cup, then add 1 crab cake and top with about a teaspoon of sauce.

Recipes with
Fruits and Vegetables

These recipes offer a lighter spread for daytime or nighttime entertaining. Their lightness, however, does not render them weak. This is a varied and flavorful collection of meat-free recipes, including Korean, Armenian, and Greek ingredients and influences.

Stuffed **Cherry 100s**

Who invented salmon mousse and why has it become the two-minute spackling compound of the catering industry? Weddings, art openings, charity fundraisers—virtually any catered event is certain to serve something filled with the stuff. Olive oil, garlic, and the herbs used here give this goat-cheese mixture an extra savory oomph. And it bears absolutely no resemblance to salmon mousse. Smart with cocktails.

Quantity: About 36 stuffed tomatoes
Total Prep Time: From 30 minutes to 1 hour, depending on how fast you can do detailed work.
Head Start: These can be stuffed 8 hours or more ahead of time and kept in the refrigerator in an airtight container.

Ingredients

* 1 to 2 pints ripe cherry tomatoes
* 8 ounces crumbly goat cheese
* 2 tablespoons extra-virgin olive oil
* 1 clove garlic, minced
* 2 tablespoons herbes de Provence
* 2 pinches kosher salt
* 1 small bunch fresh chives, cut into 1 to 1¹/₂-inch pieces
* freshly ground black pepper

Directions

Cut just less than the bottom quarter off each tomato and carefully cut and scoop out the seeds and juice. (Stuffing the tomatoes upside down like this will provide them with a flat base and prevent them from rolling off the serving plate.)

In a bowl, mash together the cheese, oil, garlic, herbs, and salt with a fork until coarsely mixed but slightly smooth. Press the goat-cheese mixture into each hollowed tomato with the end of a butter knife. Stab with a couple of chive spears and top with a half pinch of pepper. Serve chilled or at room temperature.

Note:
Herbes de Provence is a dried herb mixture that can be found in the spice section of many large grocery stores and specialty food shops.

Shorthand Dolmas

As anyone who knows her will tell you, my mom is a great gal. Those very same people will also agree that she isn't known best for her cooking. If it didn't come in a can or frozen in a box, chances were it wasn't served at our house. Her dolmas—the rolled, stuffed grape leaves attributed to Armenian, Greek, and Lebanese cuisines—are no exception, but are significantly more successful than some of her other culinary efforts. Traditionally, Armenian dolmas are filled with seasoned lamb, but my mom, true to form, uses boxed tabouli mix for her filling. Nonetheless, she never ceases to get raves for her signature dish.

Quantity: 15 to 20 dolmas

Total Prep Time: The tabouli should sit overnight in the refrigerator before using. The dolmas can be rolled in about 1 hour.

Head Start: The dolmas can be made a day or two ahead and kept refrigerated in an airtight container. Bring to room temperature before serving.

Ingredients

* One 6-ounce box tabouli (plus the olive oil and fresh tomato required to prepare the mix)
* Juice of 1 lemon
* Salt and freshly ground black pepper
* One 8 1/2-ounce jar grape leaves packed in vinegar brine (available in the ethnic section of a good supermarket or a gourmet grocer or Middle Eastern deli)
* Olive oil, for pan

Directions

Prepare the tabouli mix according to the directions on the box, adding the lemon juice and salt and pepper to taste. Refrigerate, covered, for at least 2 hours but ▶

optimally overnight, so the water and lemon juice are completely absorbed.

Rinse the grape leaves twice in a large bowl of very warm water and drain. Place a leaf flat on a work surface, vein-side up, with the stem pointing at 6:00. Snip off the stem. Place a heaping fork-ful of the tabouli filling in the center of the leaf, just above the point where the stem was trimmed. Form the tabouli horizontally into a compact, cylindrical, thumb-sized mound (see the illustration on page 63). Roll much like you would a burrito: Start by bringing the left and right edges of the leaf to the center, over the mound of filling, to form 2 straight vertical folds. Pull the rounded bottom folds up over the filling, and then roll tightly along the remaining length of the leaf. When finished, it should look like a little cigar. Repeat with the remaining leaves and filling.

Preheat the oven to 325°F. Lightly coat the bottom of a baking pan with olive oil. Place the dolmas in the pan, snugly, side by side and stacked if necessary. Add water to about $1/4$ inch deep. Cover the pan tightly with foil and bake 1 hour, or until fragrant and most of the water has evaporated. Allow to cool, covered. Serve at room temperature.

Herbed Feta Salad
in Cucumber Cups

Here is freshness worth a second cup. These lip-smacking little salads are alive with a classic Greek combination of herbs, cucumber, and feta. Very little effort is required for their impressive presentation, and an advance prep makes them easy to serve.

Quantity: About 16 cucumber cups
Total Prep Time: 45 minutes
Head Start: The cucumber cups and salad can be made up to 2 hours before serving, stored separately in airtight containers and refrigerated.

Ingredients

* 2 large cucumbers
* 1 large plum tomato, seeded and diced
* $1/4$ small red onion, minced
* 1 tablespoon chopped fresh cilantro leaves
* 3 tablespoons chopped fresh mint leaves
* 1 tablespoon freshly squeezed lemon juice
* 1 tablespoon extra-virgin olive oil
* $1/8$ teaspoon freshly ground black pepper
* $1/2$ teaspoon kosher salt
* $1/3$ cup firm feta cheese, drained, patted dry, and diced
* Cilantro leaves, for garnish

Directions

Lightly peel the cucumbers to remove only the thin outer layer of skin. With straight slices, cut off $1/2$ inch or so from each end, then cut into $1^{1}/4$-inch slices. With a small melon baller, scoop out the center of each slice to create cups.

In a nonreactive bowl 📖, combine all the remaining ingredients except the cilantro, gently spooning in the cheese last. Spoon a heaping teaspoon of the salad into each cup, and top with a cilantro leaf.

Kimchi

It's not what you'd typically classify as party food, but kimchi's tart and hot flavor, crunchy texture, and advance preparation make it a tasty and convenient accompaniment to cocktails. It's also a colorful addition to party fare when served in sake cups or small rice bowls with chopsticks. There are a multitude of Korean kimchi recipes out there, varying widely by region. This is a modified version from South Korea (the original is hotter than hell).

Quantity: Depending on portions, 20 or more servings

Total Prep Time: A long time. More than you'll want to spend. Four hours. The advantage here is that it can be prepped days and days ahead and will keep even longer.

Head Start: You can make this even before you've set a party date. Kimchi will keep up to 2 or 3 months if kept refrigerated in an airtight container. The flavor will mellow over time. This kimchi is considered "ripe" after about 2 days, but tastes great fresh. The longer it sits, the more sour the flavor.

Ingredients

* 2 heads green cabbage
* 2 cups sea salt
* 1/2 cup crushed red chili pepper flakes
* 1 teaspoon sugar
* 2/3 cup minced garlic
* 1/4 cup minced fresh ginger
* 1/2 cup sesame seeds
* 1 large white onion
* 2 carrots, peeled
* 1 small bunch mustard greens
* 10 green onions
* 10" bamboo skewers (optional, see note)

Directions

Trim the stems and outer wilted leaves of the cabbages, slicing the rest of the leaves into thin strips (about 1/4 inch), and rinsing them in cold water. Place the shredded cabbage in a large non-reactive bowl and cover with the sea salt. Let sit for about 1 hour. Toss the cabbage once or twice and allow to sit for an additional 1 to 2 hours, or until it gets soft. Rinse and drain.

In a small bowl, combine the red pepper flakes, sugar, garlic, ginger, and sesame seeds.

Slice the white onion into small to medium strips. Slice the carrots into thin medallions. Cut the mustard greens and green onions into sections 1 to 2 inches long.

In a large bowl, combine all the prepared vegetables with the spice mixture and toss. Add the drained cabbage and toss again. Store in a glass or ceramic jar, tightly covered, in the refrigerator.

Note:

For utensil-free serving, slice vegetables into pieces large enough to curl and skewer prior to salting.

Stuffed Anaheim Chilies

A stuffing of white onion, carrot, ricotta, and Jack cheese gives these mild peppers a satisfying slug to the gut. A great complement to high-octane libations.

Quantity: 15 to 20 stuffed chilies
Total Prep Time: 45 minutes
Head Start: The stuffing mixture can be prepared earlier in the day and kept covered and refrigerated. If prepared ahead of time, it may be necessary to drain the mixture before using.

Ingredients

* 12 ounces Jack cheese, grated
* 30 ounces ricotta cheese
* 1 egg
* 1 carrot, peeled and grated
* $1/2$ white onion, grated
* Scant $1/2$ teaspoon chili powder
* $1/4$ teaspoon freshly ground black pepper
* Canola oil cooking spray, for pan
* Five 4-ounce cans whole Anaheim chili peppers (these can be found in the Mexican section of large grocery stores)
* 8 ounces pepper Jack cheese, grated
* 1 teaspoon paprika

Directions

In a bowl, blend the grated Jack and ricotta cheeses, then beat the egg into the mixture. In a food processor, combine the carrot, onion, chili powder, black pepper, and the cheese mixture and process until smooth.

Preheat the oven to 325°F and lightly coat a baking sheet with cooking spray. Drain the canned chili peppers and pat dry. Using a sharp knife, make an incision halfway through the stem end of each pepper, creating an opening through which to stuff the filling, being careful not to slice off the end of the pepper completely. Using a small spoon or the tip of a butter knife, stuff each pepper full of the cheese mixture and place on the prepared baking sheet. Sprinkle the peppers with the grated pepper jack cheese, making sure the cheese covers the sliced end of each pepper (it will serve as a "glue" to seal the opening). Bake for 25 minutes. Remove from the oven and top each with a pinch of paprika. Serve warm or at room temperature.

Stuffed Zucchini Cups

Like cucumber, zucchini slices make a popular cup for salad mixtures. Though the ingredients are simple enough, the presentation of these cups and the added unexpected zing from the lemon zest and white balsamic vinegar command special attention.

Quantity: 18 zucchini cups
Total Prep Time: 30 minutes
Head Start: Pine nuts can be toasted and kept in an airtight container several days in advance. Once prepared, the cups can sit at room temperature for 1 hour or so before serving.

Ingredients

* 3 small to medium zucchini (ideally measuring about 1 1/2" in diameter)
* 3 tablespoons chopped fresh basil
* 1 tablespoon chopped fresh flat-leaf parsley
* 1/4 cup diced roasted red pepper
* 3 ounces crumbly goat cheese
* 1/4 cup pine nuts, toasted (see page 84)
* 3 tablespoons white balsamic vinegar
* 1 heaping tablespoon lemon zest (see Note, page 77)
* Freshly ground black pepper

Directions

Slice off both ends of the zucchini and cut into 1 1/4" slices. With a small melon baller, scoop out the center of each slice to create cups. Wrap the cups in batches inside 2 layers of very damp paper towels, making sure that the zucchini is covered completely, and cook in a microwave for 1 to 2 minutes, just long enough to steam the zucchini without making the pieces limp or shriveled. (Test 1 or 2 pieces first to get a better idea of microwave timing.) Remove cups from the paper towels immediately and let cool on a dry work surface or plate.

Gently toss together the basil, parsley, and red pepper in a bowl. Add the goat cheese last and fold together until evenly mixed. Spoon the mixture into each zucchini cup and top with 4 or 5 pine nuts. Drip a scant 1/2 teaspoon vinegar (more or less to taste—it packs a punch) over the top. Finish with a pinch of lemon zest and a quarter twist of the pepper mill. Transfer to a serving plate and serve at room temperature.

Orange and Black Olive Bruschetta

These colorful bites deliver cool tastes for a hot night. The salt from the cured olives, the subtle hint of chili pepper, and the juicy sweetness from the orange slices and fresh herb leaves causes such a sensory overload that upon first taste, some people have been known to actually see God.

Quantity: 20 servings
Total Prep Time: 20 minutes, plus 1 hour to refrigerate
Head Start: The salad should be made at least 1 hour ahead. The baguette can be sliced and toasted the night before and kept in an airtight container. The finished bruschetta can sit at room temperature for 1 hour before serving.

Ingredients

Topping

* 2 very ripe large oranges
* 3 tablespoons oil-cured black olives, pits removed and chopped
* $1/4$ cup finely chopped red onion
* 2 tablespoons chopped fresh basil or mint
* 1 small pinch crushed red chili pepper flakes
* $1/4$ teaspoon salt

* One 25" traditional white baguette (or two smaller baguettes)
* $1/4$ cup basil oil, for brushing (see Note)
* Freshly ground black pepper

Directions

To make the topping, with a very sharp knife, carefully slice away the peel and pith from the oranges. While holding one orange at a time over a small nonreactive bowl 📓, section it by cutting just inside the membrane. Cut each section into 5 or 6 pieces crosswise (so that each small piece has a triangular shape). Mix the oranges with the remaining topping ingredients, cover, and refrigerate for about 1 hour to let the flavors blend.

Preheat the oven to 400°F. With a sharp bread knife, cut the baguette diagonally into thin slices (just less than $1/2$ inch thick). Place the slices on a baking sheet and toast for 4 minutes on each side. Remove the slices from the oven, give one side of each a thin brushing of basil oil, then cover with a heaping mound of the orange salad, being sure to include a mixture of all the ingredients on each slice. Top each mound with a small pinch of black pepper.

Note:

Basil oil can be found in the gourmet section of many large grocery stores.

Spanakopita Puffs

The finished product is impressive and looks like hours went into its preparation, but in actuality this is one of the simplest hors d'oeuvre recipes there is. Spanakopita is generally appreciated across the board, and these bites—considerably smaller than traditional spanakopita—make for perfect party fare.

Quantity: About 36 puffs
Total Prep Time: 40 minutes
Head Start: The spinach should be drained and thawed before you begin. To make things easier, buy precrumbled feta. Otherwise, there is no prep required for these ingredients. The filled puffs shouldn't sit too long before serving—30 minutes to 1 hour at the most—or they will become soggy.

Ingredients

Filling

* 2 tablespoons olive oil
* 1 small white onion, diced
* One 10-ounce package frozen chopped spinach, thawed and drained
* $1/2$ cup crumbled feta cheese
* $1/8$ teaspoon freshly ground black pepper
* 1 tablespoon dried oregano

* Canola oil cooking spray, for pan
* $1/2$ cup water
* 1 small pinch kosher salt
* $1/4$ cup butter
* $1/2$ cup all-purpose flour
* 2 eggs

Directions

To make the filling, in a large skillet, heat the oil over medium heat; add the onion and sauté until tender. Add the spinach, feta, pepper, and oregano and stir together until well blended and heated throughout. Remove from the heat and set aside.

Preheat the oven to 425°F and lightly coat a baking sheet with cooking spray. In a saucepan, bring the water to a boil. Add the salt and butter, and stir until the butter melts. Add the flour and stir hard with a wooden spoon until the dough forms into a firm ball. Remove from the heat and let stand for 5 minutes. Add 1 egg and beat well into the dough. Add the second egg and beat again until the dough becomes stiff.

Using a teaspoon, scoop small mounds of the dough onto the prepared baking sheet, spacing them about 2 inches apart. Bake for 20 minutes, or until crisp; when removed from the oven, the puffs should hold their shape. Lightly poke each puff with a toothpick to release steam, and let cool.

Once cooled, slice the puffs in half, fill with a teaspoon of the spinach mixture, and cap.

Trough Foods

When you're aiming to please taste buds and fill stomachs with the least amount of fuss, trough foods are the easy way out. Dumped into big bowls, piled onto trays, and heaped atop serving platters, this is the party fare known to reduce even the most refined guests to barnyard hogs.

Shrimp Cocktail **Ménage à Quad**

When in doubt, say it with shrimp. Shrimp is the perfect party food: They come with their own handle, you can sauce them a million different ways, they look great in a pile, and unless your friends are a bunch of vegans, there are never, ever, any left over. Who cares if they are the cockroaches of the sea, they're still the ultimate party food!

Quantity: 16 to 20 servings (approximately 5 large shrimps per guest.)

Total Prep Time: 15 to 20 minutes for each sauce

Head Start: The shrimp can be purchased precooked, peeled, and deveined. You can rinse and drain them early in the day; cover tightly and store in the refrigerator. All the sauces can be made a day or two ahead. The peanut sauce will thicken considerably when refrigerated and should be reheated (in the microwave is fine) and stirred before serving.

For all 4 Sauces

* 2 pounds cooked shrimp with tails intact, peeled, deveined, rinsed, and thoroughly drained

Indonesian Peanut Sauce

A sauce similar to that served with satay in Thai restaurants, it's rich, sweet, and fiery.

Ingredients

* 3 tablespoons curry paste
* ³/₄ cup all-natural extra-chunky peanut butter
* 15 ounces coconut milk
* ¹/₂ cup sugar
* 1 tablespoon white wine vinegar
* 1 teaspoon kosher salt

Directions

In a large skillet over low heat, heat the curry paste and peanut butter until warm and softened. Increase the heat to medium and stir in the coconut milk and sugar, breaking up any clumps of peanut butter as you stir. Bring to a simmer. Continue to cook at a steady simmer, stirring continuously, until the mixture has thickened and slightly reduced. Remove from the heat, add the vinegar and salt, and mix until well blended. Serve warm or at room temperature.

Green Onion and Lemon Sauce

A fresh, spirited, and light dressing (speaking in terms of taste, not calories), this sauce suits a variety of seafoods.

Ingredients

* $3/4$ cup best-quality mayonnaise
* $1/2$ cup coarsely chopped green onions
* $1/4$ cup chopped fresh flat-leaf parsley
* 1 heaping teaspoon minced fresh garlic
* 1 teaspoon lemon zest (see Note)
* 2 tablespoons freshly squeezed lemon juice
* $1/2$ teaspoon kosher salt
* $1/4$ teaspoon freshly ground black pepper

Directions

Combine all the ingredients in a food processor or blender and pulse until the mixture is blended, has thickened, and has turned a pleasing green. Avoid overmixing. Transfer to a serving dish, cover with plastic wrap, and refrigerate for at least 1 hour before serving.

Note:

When zesting lemon, scrape only the yellow outer skin of the fruit and try to avoid white pith.

Wasabi Soy Mayo

This hot and mildly bitter almond-colored sauce is atypical to a shrimp cocktail spread but is a nice complement to the flavors of the other sauces suggested here.

Ingredients

* 1 cup best-quality mayonnaise
* 2 tablespoons wasabi powder
* $1^{1}/2$ tablespoons soy sauce
* 2 tablespoons rice vinegar
* 1 teaspoon freshly squeezed lemon juice
* $1/2$ teaspoon sugar

Directions

Combine all the ingredients in a food processor or blender and process until smooth. Refrigerate for at least 30 minutes before serving.

Red Cocktail Sauce

The sauce most commonly served with boiled shrimp, this version can be made spicier or tangier with a tweaking of the horseradish or lemon juice.

Ingredients

* $1/4$ cup chili sauce
* $3/4$ cup ketchup
* 2 teaspoons horseradish
* 1 tablespoon freshly squeezed lemon juice
* $1/2$ teaspoon Worcestershire sauce
* $1/2$ teaspoon Tabasco sauce
* $1/8$ teaspoon kosher salt
* $1/8$ teaspoon freshly ground black pepper

Directions

Whisk all the ingredients together in a nonreactive bowl 🥄 until evenly blended. Refrigerate for at least 30 minutes before serving.

The low road:

Although making your own cocktail sauce can be rewarding (especially if you adjust the ingredients to get the flavor and heat you most prefer), you'll be making three of the above sauces from scratch anyway, and since there are so many great bottled red cocktail sauces available, purchasing one is a good way to save time unless you're a purist.

Peanut Butter **Cannonballs**

Important note to male hosts: If your reasons for entertaining have anything to do with a master plan of the amorous variety, you may be interested to know that there is something about the combination of peanut butter and chocolate that drives women wild. While I'm not making any promises, Peanut Butter Cannonballs have become known as the aphrodisiac of party food.

For this recipe you will be using household paraffin. This is the very same wax used on skis, surfboards, and squeaky cabinetry. It may seem odd to melt this into something you're going to eat, but paraffin is an ingredient commonly used in candy making. Not only does it give the finished product a professional sheen, it also keeps the chocolate from softening too quickly at room temperature. It isn't absolutely necessary to use paraffin here, but it will produce the best results and make the dipping process a whole hell of a lot easier.

Quantity: 15 to 20 cannonballs
Total Prep Time: 30 minutes, plus additional time to chill
Head Start: These can be made a couple of days ahead and kept refrigerated in an airtight container.

Ingredients

* 1/2 stick (4 tablespoons) butter, at room temperature
* 1 3/4 cups extra-chunky salted peanut butter
* 1 cup confectioners' sugar
* 1 1/2 cups Rice Krispies
* 1/3 bar paraffin (see Note)
* One 12-ounce package semi-sweet chocolate chips

Directions

In a large bowl, combine the butter, peanut butter, sugar, and Rice Krispies, mixing and kneading by hand until all ingredients are thoroughly blended. Refrigerate or place in the freezer until just firm. (The mixture is easiest to work with if chilled.) Roll into compact balls about 1 inch in diameter and place on waxed paper. Refrigerate until firm once again.

In a nonstick skillet, melt the paraffin slowly over very low heat, stirring with a wooden spoon. Once liquefied, add the chocolate chips, keeping the heat very low and stirring constantly until the chips have completely melted and combined with the paraffin. Turn off the burner.

Using the wooden spoon, roll each peanut butter ball in the chocolate, coating it completely, then place on a tray lined with waxed paper. Additional chocolate can be drizzled over each ball for a more decorative presentation. Refrigerate until hard.

Note:
Paraffin is carried in the baking section of most grocery stores and is generally sold in 16-ounce packages containing four 4-ounce bars. You will need only a third of one 4-ounce bar for this recipe.

Dirty Herbed Olives

Plain olives become downright enticing with a simple herb, red pepper, and garlic marinade and make a perfect accompaniment to softened Brie, crackers, and hooch.

Quantity: About 10 ounces
Total Prep Time: Only a few minutes to toss together, plus an overnighter in the frig and 3 hours in the oven
Head Start: Can be prepared 2 or 3 days in advance.

Ingredients

* 10 ounces mixed black and green olives, drained
* 3 cloves garlic, crushed and coarsely chopped
* 1 1/2 teaspoons dried Herbes de Provence (see Note, page 62)
* 3 pinches crushed red pepper flakes
* 1 1/2 tablespoons extra-virgin olive oil

Directions

In a bowl, combine all the ingredients and stir to mix thoroughly. Transfer to an airtight container and refrigerate overnight.

Preheat the oven to 225°F. Transfer the mixture to an oven-proof dish, such as a casserole or chafing dish, and bake, covered, for 3 hours. Stir the olives after each hour of baking. This dish is best when served warm or at room temperature. If the mixture is refrigerated after it's been baked, reheat at 225°F for 30 minutes before serving.

The Logistics of **Pad Party Food**

How many times have you been to a party, standing with your hors d'oeuvre plate piled with shrimp tails and olive pits and maybe a couple of items you took a bite of and didn't like, wondering where the hell you're supposed to toss this stuff now that you're done with it? Have you ever picked up something from a serving platter that stays with your fingertips in a manner you didn't anticipate and find yourself at a loss for a clean napkin? Save your guests from sour moments like these by putting a little effort into the center of party operations: the food table.

Unlike tending bar, party food is all about preproduction. Although you might find yourself in the kitchen tending to the matters of hors d'oeuvres assembly or mashing an avocado as the first guest knocks, the food table—sans food—should be the first order of business. The rest of the pieces can be placed as they ▶

Baked Garlic with Anchovy Butter

I once gluttonously consumed a variation of this inordinately rich appetizer in a Beverly Hills restaurant on a very empty stomach. Dismissing the rule of moderation and throwing caution to the wind, I impatiently wolfed down fifteen or twenty whole cloves before I realized I had made a bad choice. Moments later I broke into a cold sweat, made a mad dash for the restroom, and promptly puked my guts out. I surely impressed bystanders by marching right back to my table and wolfing down more—it was that good.

Quantity: About 15 servings
Total Prep Time: Using prepeeled cloves, 1 hour and 10 minutes. Allow more time if you're peeling the garlic yourself.
Head Start: The butter can be prepared a day ahead and kept sealed in the refrigerator.

Ingredients

* 24 large cloves garlic, peeled
* 4 teaspoons anchovy paste
* 1 stick (8 tablespoons) butter, at room temperature
* 1/2 cup extra-virgin olive oil
* 2 sourdough baguettes, sliced

Directions

Gently crush each garlic clove and spread them evenly inside a ramekin, casserole, or any other ovenproof dish that looks good enough to serve from (sized so that the garlic fits snugly inside). Mash together the anchovy paste and butter with a fork until evenly blended. Spread hunks of the anchovy butter over the garlic, drizzle with the olive oil, and cover. Place in the oven and heat to 250°F. Bake for 1 hour.

Serve warm or at room temperature with the sliced baguettes and a cheese knife for spreading.

become available, but the food table itself needs to be outfitted and ready to serve its purpose before the first platter leaves the kitchen.

* People clump wherever the food is, so when choosing a spot for it, consider which location(s) will offer guests the most room

to move. If you have the space, consider two or three different locations to keep your guests circulating.

* Ideally, everything you're serving should be represented at each food location. If someone gets caught up in a conversation near the food table on the patio,

they don't want to be told later that the best bite of the night was at the table next to the bar.

* Have more napkins on hand than you ever think your guests could possibly use in one night. At the very least, figure four paper napkins per person, and more if you're not using hors

Sweet **Satan's Seed**

This is the single most addictive trough food I have ever served at any party. People wolf this down so fiercely, it's as though they are possessed. Since it tends to get sucked up fast, you may want to double the recipe, unless you'd rather leave your guests begging for more, you devil.

Quantity: 3 cups nuts
Total Prep Time: 35 minutes
Head Start: The nuts can be made a day or two before and sealed in an airtight container. Do not refrigerate.

Ingredients

* ¼ cup honey
* 2 dried Ancho chili peppers, sliced into fine flakes with a food processor
* 2 tablespoons sugar
* 2 tablespoons olive oil
* 1 teaspoon kosher salt
* ½ teaspoon cayenne pepper
* 3 cups mixed raw nuts (ideally almonds, cashews, pecans, and walnuts)

Directions

Preheat the oven to 275°F. Place all the ingredients except the nuts in a microwavable bowl and stir to combine. Heat for a few seconds to melt the mixture into the consistency of pancake syrup. Give it another quick stir to mix well, then add the nuts, gently folding them into the glaze with a rubber spatula until completely coated. Spread the nuts in an even layer on an oiled baking sheet.

Bake for a total of 25 minutes, shifting and turning the nuts with a spatula every 8 minutes or so. Watch closely during the last few minutes of baking time, as the nuts can burn easily. Once they've burned, they will totally suck and no one will eat them. Serve warm or at room temperature.

d'oeuvres plates. Keep small stacks of napkins anywhere food is being served (as well as the bar), rather than segregating them to a big pile at one end of the table. If you're personally passing a serving tray through the room, don't neglect to offer napkins as well.

* Put hors d'oeuvres spears, skewers, and cocktail forks upright in small containers. Things like Japanese teacups work great. Be sure to select cups with enough weight that they don't topple over easily.

* Plates should be stacked near the napkins, within easy reach, with two or more stacks at staggered heights if you don't want things getting too precarious. Use bread or dessert plates for a spread of this type, favoring real over paper. A mismatched collection of thrift shop and yard sale finds will serve you well, and you'll never have to buy paper plates again. ▶

Pear and **Green Onion** Brie

Here's an easy-to-please Brie that's fabulous spread on baguette slices. This is simple to prepare ahead of time and tends to be so popular that you may want to adjust the recipe to accommodate a 2-pound Brie.

Quantity: About 20 servings
Total Prep Time: 15 minutes
Head Start: The Brie can be prepped an hour or two ahead of time and kept wrapped and refrigerated. Bring to room temperature before baking.

Ingredients

* ¼ cup pine nuts
* One 15-ounce Brie wheel
* 2 tablespoons chopped green onion
* ¼ cup dried pear, diced
* ¼ cup fresh pear, diced

Directions

Toast the pine nuts in a large skillet over medium-low heat by spreading them in a single layer and stirring frequently until fragrant and golden brown. Once brown, they're done. They burn quickly, so remove from the heat immediately and let cool.

Preheat the oven to 350°F. Cut the Brie in half horizontally and remove the top. Over the sliced top of the lower half, spread even layers of green onion, dried and fresh pear, and toasted pine nuts.

Replace the top half of the Brie, press gently into place, and bake on an ovenproof serving plate for a few minutes, checking frequently, just until the Brie is visibly soft.

The low road:
Prevent a complete Brie meltdown by heating it in the microwave 20 seconds at a time until it has softened.

* Small trash cans will aid you with postparty cleanup if placed logically adjacent to serving areas. This is all too often overlooked when people entertain, making things awkward for guests. You don't want guests leaning over a can filled with shrimp tails and wadded up dirty napkins in order to freshen a drink, but you also don't want placement so out of sight that they can't find it. Discreetly tucked just under the food table—within reach but not prominent—is optimum. If the serving area doesn't allow for trash bins, make sure you've got empty bowls for the tossing of toothpicks, pistachio shells, spent drink garnishes, shrimp tails, olive pits, and other unappetizing stuff you won't want piling up on your coffee table or the bar.

Wonton **Chips** and Ginger **Guacamole**

Guacamole—the tried-and-true party stand-by—is reborn with a blast of wasabi and the zing of pickled ginger. Your guests will lick the bowl clean, guaranteed.

Quantity: 10 to 15 servings
Total Prep Time: 20 minutes for the guac, plus an extra 20 for the chips, unless you take the low road

Head Start: The chips can be made 2 or 3 days ahead and stored in an airtight container. The guacamole can be prepared early in the day and kept refrigerated. To keep the guacamole from turning brown, include a couple of pits in the mix and cover with plastic wrap, pressing the wrap down to make contact with the surface of the guacamole.

Ingredients

Guacamole
* 6 ripe Hass avocados
* $^3/_4$ cup sweet pickled ginger
* $^3/_4$ cup plain yogurt
* 3 tablespoons wasabi powder
* 6 green onions, finely chopped
* $^1/_3$ cup freshly squeezed lime juice
* 3 teaspoons kosher salt

Chips
* Toasted sesame oil
* One 12-ounce package wonton skins
* Kosher salt
* Black sesame seeds

Directions

To make the guacamole, cut the avocados in half, remove the pits (saving 2), and scoop the avocado into a nonreactive serving bowl 🖺. Blend with a fork or potato masher to a coarse consistency.

Combine the remaining guacamole ingredients in a second nonreactive bowl and blend well until smooth. Add to the avocado and mash to the desired consistency. Add the 2 reserved pits.

Preheat the oven to 350°F and lightly coat a baking sheet with sesame oil. Slice the stack of wonton skins diagonally to create 2 triangular stacks. Separate, brush both sides of each skin with sesame oil, and place on the prepared baking sheet. The skins may be folded or curled to give them some extra appeal. Sprinkle with salt and sesame seeds, and bake for 10 minutes, or until light brown. Allow to cool completely before serving or with the guacamole.

The low road:
Bypass the whole chip-making process entirely, substituting a variety of Japanese rice crackers.

Grilled Shrimp in Lettuce Tacos
with Peanut Salsa

In this case, the classic hard taco shell is replaced with an iceberg lettuce leaf. Prepared similarly to larb (see page 55), this is a serve-yourself affair. The shrimp, salsa, and lettuce cups are presented separately, so that guests can spoon the shrimp and salsa into the leaves as they like.

Quantity: About 15 large lettuce tacos
Total Prep Time: 30 minutes
Head Start: The salsa can be prepared up to a week ahead but is best when prepared an hour or two before serving. The shrimp can be cooked earlier in the day. Refrigerate in airtight containers.

Ingredients

* 8 cloves garlic
* 3 fresh red jalapeño peppers, stemmed and seeded
* 1$\frac{1}{3}$ cups roasted, unsalted peanuts
* $\frac{3}{4}$ cup cilantro leaves
* $\frac{1}{4}$ cup freshly squeezed lime juice
* $\frac{1}{4}$ teaspoon kosher salt
* 2 pounds large fresh shrimp, peeled, deveined, and tails removed
* Olive oil cooking spray, for pan
* 2 heads iceberg lettuce
* 4 limes, cut into wedges

Directions

Mince together the garlic, jalapeños, and peanuts in a food processor. Add the cilantro and process briefly until well mixed but still coarse. Transfer to a non-reactive bowl 📖. Stir in the lime juice, salt, and just enough water (add 1 scant teaspoon at a time) to moisten the mix.

Rinse and drain the shrimp. Lightly coat a grill pan with olive oil cooking spray and heat over medium-high heat. Cook the shrimp, flipping once, until the meat turns pink, cooks through, and becomes pleasingly charred. Remove from the pan, let cool, and chop coarsely into small pieces.

Slice the stems ends off the lettuce heads and carefully peel off about 15 crisp outer leaves, being careful not to tear them. Gently rinse and dry the leaves, then pile them loosely in a shallow bowl. Serve alongside the chopped shrimp, peanut salsa, and lime wedges, all at room temperature or slightly chilled.

The **Rhythm Method** of Party Prep
A Four-Day Plan to Avoid the Unwanted

If you're throwing a party on Saturday night, you're a fool to wait until Saturday morning to pull it together. There's always more to do than you think and never enough time. The biggest disadvantage to the mad-dash approach is that you'll probably burn yourself out before the first guest arrives, which is never the optimal way to start an evening. If you spend a little time each day, starting just four days prior, you can actually pull everything together single-handedly without a sense of dread or the slightest degree of performance anxiety.

Four Days Before
Guest confirmations. If there's anyone you haven't heard from, call and get your answer. If there's anyone you wanted to invite and neglected to call the first time around, don't wait, do it now. Four days is plenty of time for a "last-minute" invitation without making the invitee feel like an afterthought. If you wait too long—like the day before the party—they're likely to be suspicious and think you're having trouble getting people to come.

    Settle on the food. Make a list of the food you plan to buy already prepared and the ingredients needed for the stuff you want to cook. Check your own cupboards against your shopping list before you head out— you probably already have a jar of cayenne pepper shoved way in the back.

Three Days Before
Inventory. Pull out your trays, bowls, and platters, and make sure you've got a dish for everything you're planning to serve. Grab your shopping list and hit the grocery store. In addition to food, consider items like skewers and toothpicks. Get more lemons and limes than you think you'll need; they will all get used. If you're serving punch and want to use an ice ring, start the freezing process now.

Two Days Before
Food prep. There's a lot you can prepare two days in advance that will hold up just fine. Hors d'oeuvre components like marinated olives, wonton cups, sauces, and spreads can be made even further in advance, and some taste better when they've had a few days to sit in the refrigerator (some recipes require that they do).

    Clean the house. Unless you are a total slob, there's no way your house will get messed up again in 48 hours. If you hate cleaning, at least cover the areas of the house where you expect guests to roam, especially the bathroom. Nail down the extras. Do you need to borrow music, chairs, glasses, or serving dishes?

One Day Before
Prep the bar. Buy ice now and stow it in the freezer to save yourself a last-minute trip to the store. Do a booze run. The rule for checking your own stock before you buy may hold for spices, chicken broth, or bread crumbs, but not hooch. No matter how much you've got, you will

always need more. If you've asked guests to bring liquor, take care of the mixers, juices, tonic, seltzer, et al., especially anything that needs to be served cold so it has time to refrigerate. Set up the bar—or the area you've designated for drink mixing—with the essentials.

Do a last shop for ingredients that require down-to-the-minute freshness like seafood and herbs. If you're type A, pick out what you're going to wear. It's not a decision that should wait until the last minute if you value your mental well-being.

The Day of the Party
The last details. Prepare the last of the food and clean up the kitchen. Make your music selections and load the CD player, or stack them in the order that you want them to be played. Stock the bathroom with clean hand towels and make sure you've got several extra rolls of toilet paper or you'll piss off the girls. Outfit an area for plates, napkins, skewers, and other food-service essentials. Cut lemon and lime wedges for the bar. Relax. Don't spend the whole day freaking out about details or you'll be a wreck before the party even starts. If you have some last-minute item you've found you're in need of, call and ask a guest who's a close friend to bring it, and pour yourself a drink.

Food Sets the Mood

Stagger the serving of your party food. Have a few simple items out as people arrive: spreads, soft cheeses, fruit, bread. As guests grow in number and get started on their first drink and some initial nibbling, hit them with platters offering the mildly amusing: shrimp, spiced nuts, dips. Once the party is close to full swing, bring out the big guns, your labor-intensive showstoppers. You'll get a very different reaction when you build to a crescendo than if you've got everything out when the first guest walks through the door. It's the difference between a stripper who takes twenty minutes to drop seven veils and a common pole dancer who takes the stage already naked. Tease your guests and build to a rousing gustatory climax.

Mood Altering

Piscatorial mood lighting puts fire in the eye and microcosmic enhancement in the room. Ceiling-suspended iconographic incense burners arouse the senses and amplify spatial dimension. An ambient video sideshow can offer a mind-bending alternative to a second-rate art collection. The best parties are their own separate reality—an evening in a psychotropic playground—and with only the slightest push, you can encourage the shift. For the talented host, a party is a production of epic proportions, including a dynamic cast, a skillfully set stage, and the groove of a judiciously selected score to underline the action.

Setting **the Mood**

A Collection of Music Suited to Score the Three Stages in the Life of a Party

Like the man behind the curtain, a host wears many hats, and playing DJ is yet another job of the behind-the-scenes variety. A careful selection of music is as important to entertaining as a good guest list. Music is your backdrop and provides the party with an identity. It has the power to set or change the mood and can give your guests subtle cues about where the evening is headed, when it has reached its peak, and when you would like everyone to get the hell out (or if you'd like them to linger until dawn).

Whether they realize it or not, your guests will respond to the lead your music provides.

By keeping a score soft, trancy, and sedate, you may inadvertently give the party an emotional ceiling. When an evening reaches its climax, simply increasing the volume of a thumping bass line or frantic mambo will grant your guests silent permission to abandon inhibition and become shamelessly flirtatious or shamefully sloppy. Music is your invisible scenery—your soundscape—and to underestimate its importance is to forfeit one of the most important tools you have to shape a party and set its tone.

For sources, see 📖 by individual title.

Music for Gearing Up

Here's a sampling of recordings perfect for the crucial period of guest arrivals, first drinks, and initial introductions.

Beat at Cinecittà
Various artists

Cinecittà is Italy's movie factory—"Hollywood on the Tiber"—having served directors like Mario Brava, Federico Fellini, and Sergio Leone. This is the music of Cinecittà, specifically the scores of their erotic, lustful, lascivious, and downright raunchy films of the 1960s and 1970s. Cool, sexy, and strange, it's an Italian treatment of pop, rock, and jazz for the jet set. This is the swankiest in upbeat sleazy listening.

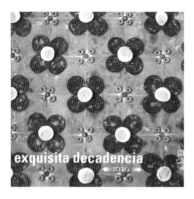

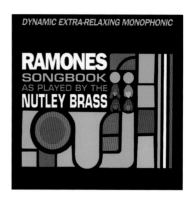

Exquisita Decadencia
Pedro Vigil

Following his extraordinary *Música Para Hacer la Digestíon,* Vigil creates another sound escape into an exotic and cinematic world of go-go tunes and smooth bossa nova. Once again we're treated to his signature palette of sound: jazzy nocturnes, velvety instrumentals, and scores of orchestral grandeur, finely crafted with an unmistakably Continental tone. Often impossible to pigeonhole: "a track for bubble baths and love scenes," "songs for devotees of leopard skins," and "elegant fashion party" are terms that have been used to describe some of the songs on *Exquisita Decadencia.* Very, very easy on the ears and, like quaaludes on the spirit.

Betty Page Danger Girl: Burlesque Music
Various artists

"Burlesque music" is somewhat of a misnomer as it's used here, in that this isn't stripper music of the bump-and-grind variety. This is, however, an impressive collection of mood and cocktail instrumentals evocative of 1950s and 1960s film noir and the black-and-white photo spreads starring the album's namesake. The orchestration runs from cool, jazzy, and smooth to torrid, feisty, and naughty, much like the music one might imagine Irving Klaw slapping on the turntable as he popped those flashbulbs. Many of the composers featured here are noteworthy for their film and television scores, which is clearly why the music has such atmosphere.

Ramones Songbook
Nutley Brass

If you're too old for the mosh pit but still like to infuse your party with a little punk rock spirit, turn yourself on to the sensational sounds of the Nutley Brass with this delightfully revamped ten-song collection of Ramones favorites. The tunes creep up on you, appreciated first only at face value, then striking a deeper chord. Though the familiar melodies of songs like "Gimme Gimme Shock Treatment" and "Teenage Lobotomy" tend to get lost among the xylophone, horns, piano, and strings, the music holds up remarkably well, to a hip-shaking, toe-tapping, head-bobbing extreme.

Music for Peaking

Play these selections when the party is in full swing and you want to do everything you can to keep it there.

The Fluid Soundbox
Stereophonic Space Sound Unlimited

A smooth, groovy, gravity-defying collection from Switzerland's greatest modern composers, whom you may never have heard of but are certain to love: Ernest Maeschi and Karen Diblitz. This adventure in instrumental space-age exotica in the tradition of classic surf and hot rod instrumentals of the 1960s incorporates organs, vibraphones, bongos, electronica, and drum loops. The team of composers is also responsible for Swiss TV's coolest theme music, as evident on their first disk, *Lost TV Themes,* another party must.

Schulmädchen Report
Gert Wilden and Orchestra

Skinny-dipping romps, horny babysitters, oversexed college coeds, randy professors, and good-natured incest: these were the themes of "The Schoolgirl Report," a series of soft-core German drive-in movies produced in the early 1970s. The most notable difference between German soft-core of the '70s and the sexploitation produced in the United States of the same period is, most unmistakably, the music. German composer Gert Wilden is responsible for the wholesome psychedelia and syrupy cocktail sounds that scored these and a number of other German films, television productions, and cabarets. This—the only CD retrospective of Wilden's film compositions—is music to swing to (in a naughty, liberated, German, free-loving, college coed sort of way). While there are a couple of lower-key tracks in the collection, the overall sound holds to an energized, sexualized, supercharged groove.

Doob Doob O'Rama, Volume 2
Various artists

A twenty-one-track collection of film scores from vintage Indian cinema: action, romance, and musical fantasy, rich with dimension and bordering on the surreal. A steady and frenetic beat sets the pace for an overtly theatrical presentation of rock 'n' roll guitar, Indian strings, grandiose orchestration, and low-end synth pop, peppered with lots of reverb. The frantic vocals interspersed with non sequitur sound bites make for an exotic, at times seductive, and thoroughly lively aural backdrop.

Asian pop and girl group exotica that's nearly impossible to classify. Twenty recordings from the 1960s and 1970s imported from Hong Kong, Korea, Malaysia, Singapore, and Japan. From go-go tracks that sound like Nancy Sinatra material to songs in a traditional vein cut with a stylized, fast-paced twist, *Asian Takeaways* promises a no-holds-barred thrill ride through a strangely cohesive collection.

to tell just exactly where the original work ends and his modification begins. On this collection, we have a soundtrack for, as the title suggests, a night at the Playboy Mansion. This is a score for the kind of abandon that only seems to happen after hours under the flashing lights of a dance floor, or by poolside on a hot summer evening among a group of attractive people with loose morals and compromised judgment. *Si non oscillas noli tintinnare.*

Asian Takeaways
Various artists
Ever heard a Chinese cha-cha? Can you handle the fuzzed-out guitars and fever-pitch vocals of Malaysia? Do you dig wild sax and guitar boogies from Korea? Does the thought of an all-girl garage band from Singapore put you in a cold sweat? This is vintage

A Night at the Playboy Mansion
Various artists; selected and remixed by Dimitri from Paris
When Dimitri gets his hands on a disco track, it's like a restoration team working on the ceiling of the Sistine Chapel; when he's done, it's nearly impossible

Pop-Shopping
Various artists
A collection of German advertising scores may not be the first thing you'd reach for when pulling together your Pad party music, but after giving *Pop-Shopping* a spin, you may never want to listen to anything else. Serving as a

precursor to television commercials, much of the music collected here was published on flexis in the 1960s and 1970s, reaching customers through the little picture disks and colorful sleeves that served as vehicles to push products. The sound is jumpy and sophisticated (vibraphones, Hammond organ, flutes, electric guitars, cool strings, and hot trumpets), in spite of the fact that the music was created to push fabric softener, Instamatic cameras, blue jeans, hair-care items, and candy bars.

His hyperstylish collage of lounge music, funky bass, bongos, Hammond organ (courtesy of Brother Cleve from Combustible Edison), and Latin-inspired percussion has fueled crowded dance floors worldwide and scored the runways for Prada, Fiorucci, and Issey Miyake, among others. The sound of Ursula 1000 is consistently easy, accessible, and infectious.

liantly demonstrating the cultural fusion of the Afro-Latin groove. To classify this collection as "cocktail music" would be demeaning, so I won't, but you'd be hard-pressed to find a more suitable score for a sophisticated night of expensive liquor, cracked ice, and 3,000 calorie hors d'oeuvres. Not one dud on the whole disk.

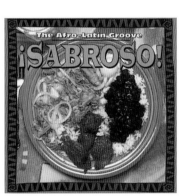

¡Sabroso!: The Afro-Latin Groove
Various artists
These eighteen sultry treasures were recorded from the late 1950s to the early 1970s, by instantly recognizable artists (like Tito Puente and Cal Tjader) and lesser-known but no less accomplished musicians, composers, and orchestra leaders, bril-

Kinda' Kinky
Ursula 1000
Transcontinental DJ Alex Gimeno is the mastermind behind the intoxicating sound of Ursula 1000, and this, his third album, ranks as an instant party music classic.

Music for Coming Down

Move on to these selections when the party has
seen its climax, but the evening is far from over.

Hava Narghile
Various artists

If Russ Meyer's *Beyond the
Valley of the Dolls* had
been shot in Istanbul, this
could have served as its score.
A twenty-one-track disc that
comes alive with the hypnotic
sounds of the electrified saz—
Turkey's national instrument
not unlike the sitar (imagine
Ravi Shankar jamming with
Dick Dale)—fuzzed-out raga
rock guitar, and a belly-dancing
beat, with most of the tunes
sung in Turkish. Mavi Isiklar,
Melih Faruk Serdar Saygun,
and Grup Bunalim may not
be names you'll hear on your
local oldies station, but if you're
inclined in the acid garage rock

way, a trip through the world
of Turkish psychedelia is one
you won't soon forget.

Crime Jazz, Music in the First Degree
Various artists

Crime drama and smooth jazz
mix like vermouth and good
gin, and this era-specific genre
of jazz is represented here
in its golden age, the 1950s and
1960s. Stan Kenton, Quincy
Jones, Count Basie, Henry
Mancini, Laurie Johnson, and a
host of other mood masters
factor into this bluesy, boozy
trip through themes and
atmospheric scores from productions like *The Wild One,*

*Johnny Staccato, Touch of
Evil, The Young Savages, Naked
City, M Squad,* and others.
It's lounge music taken to
a dangerous edge, music that
lends itself to martinis but
doesn't promise that you'll live
long enough to eat the olive.

Electronic Toys
Various artists

Mondo Moog! A supersonic syn-
thesized freak-out of electronic instrumentals from the
1970s. Many of these tracks
were stock recordings composed
for television commercials and
movies, which lends some of
them a subtle familiarity. Like
a nitrous oxide–charged ride

on an amusement park carousel, it's music that pushes the envelope to a place that's almost too trippy to travel, but the syrupy sweetness is cut with just enough acid adventure to maintain an uneasy but intriguing balance.

Mystic Groove
Various artists
Mystic Groove is a haunting, pulsating, electronic meditation for the twenty-first century. Hypnotic and dreamy without being somnolent, this is the perfect music for easing into an after-party, a postparty *pad de deux,* or the thankless and unavoidable collecting of empty highballs and dirty hors d'oeuvres plates after the last guest has said goodbye. This unusual collection features original and

remixed recordings of Indian, Turkish, and Arabic origin, smoothly woven together into one mystical, moody magic-carpet ride.

Circus of Life
Jean-Jaques Perrey
"Many people . . . thought I was dead," Jean-Jaques Perrey says in the liner notes of his first U.S. release since his electronic opus *Moog Indigo* in 1970, "but as you can see and hear, I am still alive doing crazy music." And crazy it is. An exciting advent for Perrey fans, his new CD is, by his own account, "electro-pop-easy-listening" and remains unfailingly true to his signature style. For those unfamiliar with the music of Jean-Jaques Perrey, however, the term "easy listening" needs qualification.

For some, his music has the same effect as twelve cups of strong black coffee and half a pack of cigarettes. That said, *Circus of Life* is the most accessible collection of Perrey recordings to date. And it is very circuslike, albeit a circus seen through a kaleidoscopic lens at the bottom of the rabbit hole. This is a drugs-without-drugs experience, strangely timeless, of ambiguous origin, and pleasantly disorienting.

Paris Combo
Paris Combo
This French quintet has been called the sexiest, smartest, and most invigorating band to hop the Atlantic. Their exciting blend of modern flamenco, gypsy, jazz, swing, blues, and the chanson music of France is almost too good to be true,

transporting you to places you never knew you wanted to go. Both delicate and powerful as only a female Parisian knows how, chanteuse extraordinaire Belle du Barry handles the fusion of Old World cabaret with New World punch like a seasoned dominatrix wielding a rider's crop. Don't mistake their treatment of Parisian cabaret as retro, this is the cabaret of the new millennium. There is absolutely no way for Paris Combo to disappoint. Your guests will thank you.

Swingin' Singles: Cocktail Mix Volume 3
Various Artists

"Swingin'" as in "with it," not "wife swapper" the liner notes are quick to confirm, number three in Rhino's popular Cocktail Mix compilations,

Swingin' Singles is an obvious choice for party tunes. Here we have the old standbys, Sammy Davis Jr., Dean Martin, and Mel Tormé, but without being hit over the head with clichés common among so many other collections of this ilk. A careful seasoning of unexpected cuts from vocalists like Sarah Vaughn, Eartha Kitt, and Diana Dors, along with some wonderful orchestration by Stan Kenton, Henry Mancini, and Don Ralke give this collection an unpredictable blend. The overall mood of the collection is playful, humored, unmistakably dated, and at times even comic, but it never feels ridiculous.

Put a Flavor to Love
Janet Klein & her Parlor Boys

She's the toast of Tokyo, the sweetheart of the silent movie house set, and the darling of the old-time dance halls—and if her name is unfamiliar, you'd do very well to give this pint-sized ukulele lady a look-see. Through this beguiling assortment of hot swing, French ballads, early jazz, obscure novelty tunes, and arcane Vitaphone numbers, Janet serves as our musical EMT, resuscitating life into material lost from disintegrating celluloid, banned from the radio, or curtailed by limited test pressings. Using dance halls, old rehearsal spaces, or anyplace she and the boys can find toasty acoustics, Janet's vocal frosts an ample sampling of rarities like the mandocello, xylophone, ocarina, lap steel guitar, accordion, and even the washboard and singing saw!

Goldfish Globule
Candlelight Lantern

Like a living lava lamp, this simple assembly produces trance-inducing effects—especially after a couple of drinks..

Tools

* Glass cleaner
* Paper towels
* Large mug or teacup
* Narrow kitchen tongs
* Extra-long fireplace matches

Supplies

* 8" clear glass hurricane lamp flue
* 8" clear or smoked glass ceiling light globe
* Clear silicone aquarium sealant
* 3 equal-length brass plumber's chains (also called safety chains), cut to desired measurement
* 3 brass split key rings, two 1" and one 1½"
* 1 pound aquarium gravel
* Aquarium accoutrements
* Small tapered candle
* 1 or 2 goldfish
* Swag ceiling hook

Directions

1. Thoroughly clean and dry the glass flue and the inside of the glass light globe.

2. Coat the bottom lip of the flue (the larger end) with silicone sealant and place inside the glass globe, centered, so that the silicone-coated lip of the flue meets the bottom of the globe and creates a seal. Sit upright inside the mug or teacup to hold the globe stationary, and let sit ▶

Working the Room

First and foremost, parties are about people engaging with other people, and a successful social atmosphere can depend entirely on whether or not you, as host, make a conscious effort to cultivate one. Beyond duties like hanging coats and pouring drinks lies a realm of distinctions that often eludes even a seasoned host.

A party begins with the first introduction.

The talent for making introductions seems to have become a lost art, which is unfortunate because it can be the determining factor for whether or not your guests really enjoy your party. It's an enormous disappointment for a guest to walk through the door and receive only a quick welcome, direction to the food table, and a drink, then to be left on their own in a room filled with people they've never met. The daunting chore of folding yourself into the social mix without any help from the host is one of the reasons so many people dread going to parties. Everyone wants to feel included, so make it easy for them. ▶

until sealant is completely set, about 48 hours.

3. Make the suspension chain by connecting one looped end from each chain to a 1" key ring. Counting from the linked ring, connect the $1\frac{1}{2}$" ring through the loop of the 28th link of each chain. This assembly will provide a cradle for the globe to sit in and cinch the chains together just above the mouth of the globe.

4. To finish the top of the suspension chain, loop the end of each link through the second 1" ring.

5. Once the silicone has set, fill the globe with gravel and aquarium accoutrements. Include a bed of gravel at the bottom of the flue in which the candle can be held stationary. Fill the ball with water (keeping the flue interior dry) and insert the candle into the flue using the kitchen tongs. Slip the goldfish into the water, being very careful to avoid tossing it into the dry flu—otherwise, you'll have to dump the whole thing out and you will have a miserable half-dead fish covered in gravel.

6. Since the final assembly is somewhat precarious should it get knocked into, place the swag hook above an area clear of party traffic and reasonably out of reach. Hang the chain, and place the ball so that each chain divides the globe in thirds, providing the best cradle (best done with two people).

7. Use the extra-long fireplace matches to light the candle, avoiding contact with the chain.

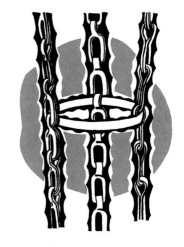

Note:
The ideal water temperature for goldfish is between 60 and 65°F. They can tolerate warmer water, but the candle shouldn't remain lit to the point that it warms the water beyond normal room temperature. The Globule Candlelight Lantern should serve only as a temporary home for any goldfish.

Cross-reference.
In addition to introducing people, create a link. Give them something to talk about: acknowledge parallel interests, histories, or fields of work. This may feel tedious and perfunctory, but it's the most effective way to establish connectedness and get people engaged. And don't think reference points need to be safe or dignified: If there are two people in the room who don't know each other yet who both fronted failed punk bands in the 1980s, your segue is waiting for you. It also isn't necessary to take the path of least resistance. A host with a keen judge of character knows how to aim for a more dynamic connection by introducing two people that would never otherwise cross paths in their lifetimes, sometimes with surprising results.

Make every guest the guest of honor.
When someone new arrives, excuse yourself from whatever activity you may currently be engaged in and make a point to offer a sincere welcome. Take their coat, serve them a drink, offer them a bite, and make some key introductions. Even though you may have a list of other duties to tend to, it's important to spend

Bibliophilic Stash Box

Maybe you need a place to hide your smokes from a suspecting spouse. Maybe you're looking for a place to stow a good bottle of whiskey, just in case. Maybe you're sick and tired of your housemates pinching your expensive Moroccan saffron. Maybe a box of condoms, a bottle of lube, and whatnot on the table next to your bed could be contained a bit more discreetly. Whatever you might want to keep hidden throughout the week but share during party time (or use throughout the week and hide during party time), here's a good place for it.

Tools

* One or more C-clamp vises
* Rubber bands
* Electric drill with $5/16$" and $7/32$" drill bits
* Coping saw
* X-acto knife

Supplies

* 2 wood templates, sized accordingly (see step 1)
* Hardcover book, 400 or more pages in length (see Note)
* Two $8/32$" x $1^1/2$" aluminum binding posts and screws
* All-purpose glue
* Felt or cardboard (optional)

Directions

1. First create 2 wood templates with an overall measurement about $1^1/2$" smaller than the trim size of the book pages.

2. Starting from the final page in the book, sandwich $1^1/2$" of pages between the templates. Center the templates on the pages and vice into place. Secure the remaining loose pages to the cover with rubber bands to keep them out of the way as you work.

3. Drill $5/16$" holes through the viced pages at the point of each corner of the template.

4. Unfasten the blade of the coping saw and slip the blade through ▶

some time with each guest and to give them your undivided attention while you do so, even if only for a few minutes. Ignoring a guest, even inadvertently, is a party faux pas of the most egregious sort.

Do some social trouble-shooting.

There seems to be at least one at every party: someone who, for one reason or another, is best taken in small doses. It's important to know when your party requires a little damage control. If you see a guest turning to stone at the receiving end of an unrelenting one-sided conversation, or eye an overzealous inebriate becoming insufferably flirtatious with someone too polite for their own good, it's up to you to know when to step in and gracefully sacrifice yourself for the well-being of your guests.

Be your own busboy/girl.

A partyscape littered with dirty hors d'oeuvres plates and a collection of highballs marked with lipstick stains is not festive. Sitting at a coffee table covered with party debris and abandoned garnishes does not encourage guests to linger. If you spot a spent cocktail glass, remove it from the scene. If a platter of food has long been picked over, ▶

a drilled hole. Reattach the blade and cut along the outside edge of your template, sawing a straight line connecting each drilled hole. Depending on the size of the book, it may become necessary to unfasten and reattach the coping saw blade for better positioning as you work. You will also need to shift the vice once or twice to allow clearance for the saw.

5. Discard the core of the pages and brush away all paper dust. With the book open on your work surface, position the cavity pages of the book so that they are aligned squarely, as they would be if the book were closed. Press the pages securely in place and drill a $7/_{32}$" hole, centered, on the left and right borders of the cavity pages, passing through the back

cover. (Use your templates as a protective work surface to prevent drilling into your tabletop.) Insert the binding posts and screws to secure the pages into place.

6. To hide the binding posts, slice into the center of the page preceding the first cavity page with an X-acto knife, and fold the cut edges of that page into the cavity for a finished edge. Glue into place. You can further finish the cavity by lining it with felt or cardboard, glued into place.

Note:
To locate an affordable hardcover book of great length, I suggest you hit a good used bookstore and look for almost any title by Stephen King or James Michener. For the very frugal, hit a yard sale

between noon and 2:00 p.m. when King and Michener titles are practically given away. As a last resort, *The Complete Works of William Shakespeare* is an excellent book for this project— you'll never get around to reading all those sonnets anyway.

take it to the kitchen. The trick here is to keep the room looking smart while remaining discreet. If guests sense that you're trying to clean up, they may volunteer to help. This is not the objective.

Make the winning refill.
Moving to the bar to get a drink refilled is always an easy way out for a guest who wants to make a social transition, but stepping

in and offering to refresh a drink for someone with an empty glass is one of the most charming services a host can provide.

Ask yourself: Is everyone having a great time except me?
Remember your reasons for throwing the party in the first place. As host, know that your evening will be interrupted a million times

for the above reasons, but don't allow yourself to get so preoccupied with the details of event management that you lose the important balance between working the party and working the room. A wise host never clears a dirty plate at the expense of their own good time.

Puckery Accent Swags

Green florist vases—the hallmark of the American thrift store. Like Shawn Cassidy records, their omnipresence serves as a sad reminder that some castoffs never find a second home, that one's person's junk is not always another person's treasure, that not every piece of trash in this world can be recycled . . . or can it?

Who would have dreamt that the unassuming vase that stirs repugnance in nearly everyone actually makes for festive party lighting when suspended upside down? Challenging on the mind at first perhaps, but after you've grooved on their mellow gleam for a time, you won't even see the vase anymore, per se. Its abrasiveness is reborn in a new post-postmodern light.

Tools

* Electric drill
* $1/2$" glass and tile drill bit
* Protective eyewear
* Wire strippers
* Phillips screwdriver

Supplies

* Green florist vase
* Lamp cord (cut to desired length)

* Keyless shell light socket
* One $1^{1}/_{2}$" $^{1}/_{8}$ IP threaded steel nipple
* One 1" $^{1}/_{8}$ IP brass washer
* One $^{3}/_{4}$" $^{1}/_{8}$ IP brass locknut
* 1" diameter female decorative brass loop for ceiling fixtures
* Swag ceiling hook
* Swag chain
* Easy-wire plug
* Line switch (optional)

Directions

1. Place the vase bottom-side up on a secure work surface that will prevent the vase from slipping while being drilled (such as a rubber doormat, scrap of carpet, or piece of heavy cardboard). Mark the center spot, put on your protective eyeware, and drill a hole just large enough to allow the threaded nipple to pass through. ▶

Do's and Don'ts:
How to be a Model Guest

What follows is a discussion of some of the finer points that distinguish the well socialized from the clueless: All you really need to know to win future party invitations.

Do ask if there's anything you can bring when you receive an invitation. Your host will probably say no, but you'll still enjoy the advantage of looking like a genuinely considerate person.

Do r.s.v.p. It's only decent to call and let your host know if you'll be able to show up or not. If you earn yourself the reputation of a no-show, your host may (justifiably) exclude you from future events.

Don't ever pick at, squeeze, or pop anything on your face while getting ready for a party. Whatever you think you can do to minimize a blemish in fifteen minutes or less won't work. You know this.

Do bring a small gift, flowers, or a bottle of hooch—it says that you, as a guest, mean business, that you're not a freeloader, that you have class. (Etiquette says ▶

Only apply pressure to start the initial drilling and to keep the drill bit from slipping. Once the hole has been started, let the drill do the work. Applying pressure is almost certain to cause the vase to shatter, destroying your worthless find. Be cautious around the bit itself—it will get burning hot.

2. Once the hole is finished, clean the vase with warm soapy water, rinse, and dry.

3. Separate the two wires at the cut end of the lamp cord so that each separate wire measures about $1^1/_2$" in length. Using the wire strippers, trim off enough of one wire casing to expose about a 1" length of the wire. Twist the exposed copper strands of wire into a thin cable to prevent fraying.

Repeat with the other separated end.

4. Light sockets come apart in three pieces: the bottom cup, the interior mechanism, and the metal sleeve. Screw the threaded nipple into the bottom cup of the socket set (you may need to remove a small screw from the side of the cup's threaded interior). Slip the end of the prepared lamp cord through the threaded nipple and bottom cup assembly. Loop each end of the exposed lamp wire clockwise around each (loosened) terminal screw on the interior mechanism. The wire coming from the *ribbed* side of the cord gets connected to the *silver* terminal screw, and the remaining *smooth* wire gets connected to the *brass* terminal screw. Tighten the screws

to hold the wires securely in place, slide the insulated metal sleeve over the interior mechanism, and snap together.

5. Run the opposite cut end of the lamp cord through the inside of the vase and out the drilled hole. Slide the washer and lock-nut over the cut end of the lamp wire down to the drilled hole. Bring the threaded nipple up through the drilled hole, top with the washer, and fasten with the locknut.

6. Slide the brass loop over the cut end of the wire to meet the threaded nipple, and screw securely into place. Attach your swag chain, and thread the lamp cord through the links. Finish the lamp by attaching the plug, and a line switch, if you like.

---

that your gift be for the host, not the party, so don't be surprised if your host puts it aside for later.)

Do call before you leave for the party to ask your host if they have any last minute needs, but only if the host is a close friend. You may be the one forced to drink gin and tonic at room temperature later in the evening because the host ran short on ice.

Do dress for the occasion. If the party is dress-up, then dress up. No one has given you diplomatic fashion immunity.

Don't bring along uninvited guests or anyone under legal age unless you call first and get permission from your host. If you do call for permission, make it easy for your host to say no—they might have a social plan that

doesn't include your visiting sister and her three teenaged sons.

Don't ever bring a dog to a party. Many pet owners are a little out of touch when it comes to making this distinction, but dogs are not people. Unless your dog can hold a cocktail, carry on an interesting conversation, and look good in a sharkskin suit and a skinny tie, leave it at home.

Opium Den Incense Burner

Engage the senses, embellish your atmosphere, and dazzle guests by transforming a cheap cone of incense into a veritable religious experience with this ridiculously simple assembly of terra-cotta saucers, wood beads, a bit of hardware, and a scrap of fussy textile.

Tools

* Ruler
* Felt marker or pencil
* Electric drill
* $3/16$" and $3/8$" masonry drill bits
* Paper towels or clean rags
* Newspaper
* Matches

Supplies

* 2 terra-cotta plant saucers, one 6" and one $63/4$"
* Thick paper, for template
* Metallic gold spray paint
* Nine $8/32$" hex nuts
* Twelve #8 washers
* Three $8/32$ x 12" threaded rods
* Wood beads
* One $3/4$" $1/8$ IP brass locknut
* One $1/2$" $1/8$ IP threaded steel nipple
* One 1" $1/8$ IP brass washer
* 1" diameter female decorative brass loop for ceiling fixtures
* Three $8/32$" brass acorn nuts
* Swag ceiling hook
* Swag chain
* Statue, standing 10" or smaller
* About 1 cup sand or gravel
* Incense cone

Directions

1. Start by placing the smaller terra-cotta saucer inside the larger one. Make a triangular paper template of equal 4" sides. Center the template inside the smaller saucer and mark all 3 points on the saucer with a sharp felt marker or pencil.

2. While holding them securely in place, slowly drill through both saucers at each marked point with the $3/16$" bit. ▶

Don't light up if you don't see an ashtray. Even the coolest non-smoking hosts don't want their living room to smell like a bowling alley. Always ask first, or go outside for a spell.

Do use a coaster or a cocktail napkin when you set down your drink, even if your host has what looks like crummy furniture. It's the courteous thing to do.

The mark you leave on a party shouldn't be on the credenza.

Don't show up late and expect to be fed. Know that food is the first thing to go. Learn to settle for platter scrapings or eat something before you arrive. And never ask for something to eat if it hasn't been offered. The host wants to have a good time, too, not serve as a short-order cook.

Do call the day after, or send a card or e-mail to say thank you and tell your host what a great time you had, even if you didn't. They put forth a lot of effort to show you a good time, and receiving these kinds of phone calls makes the host's day-after cleanup a lot less thankless.

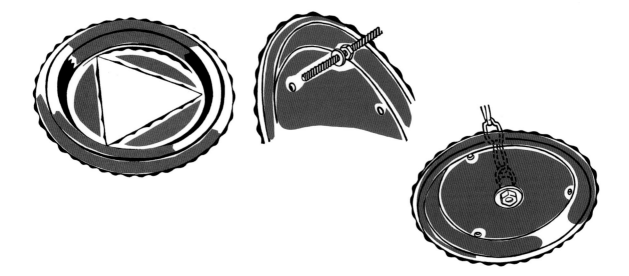

3. Separate the saucers. Use the ruler to find the center of the smaller saucer, and mark it. Drill a hole on that spot with the ³/₈" bit.

4. Clean the saucers of dust with a damp cloth and let dry.

5. With the saucers lying face up on newspaper, spray them with the metallic gold paint. Spray several light coats, allowing each coat to dry before applying the next, until you've achieved solid and complete coverage. Once dry, flip the saucers and paint the underside of each the same way.

6. Thread a hex nut and a #8 washer down about 1" onto one

end of each 12" rod. With the larger saucer face up, slip the 1" tip end of one rod threaded with a nut down through each drilled hole of the saucer. From the underside of the saucer, thread a #8 washer and a hex nut at the very bottom of the rod. Tighten down the washer and hex nut from the top side and secure each rod into place.

7. String the rods with beads, leaving about ¹/₂" of the top of the rod exposed.

8. Thread a #8 washer and a hex nut down over the bare ends of the rods to meet the top bead of each, and tighten into place.

9. Thread the locknut onto the bottom of the threaded nipple. Slip the nipple up through the center hole on the concave side of the smaller saucer, and cap the other side with the 1" brass washer and the female brass loop.

10. Slide the holes of the smaller saucer down over the ends of the three rods, and secure in place with a washer and an acorn nut on each.

11. Secure the swag hook. Attach the swag chain to the top loop and suspend from the ceiling. Position the statue, add the sand or gravel to the bottom of the lower dish, position the incense cone, and light.

Eye Candy Land:

A Sampling from the Optic Hors d'Oeuvres Tray

A video at a party is like a go-go dancer at a bar: It isn't necessary for them to command everybody's undivided attention to provide entertainment. Party videos serve only to further embellish the visual atmosphere of your party scene. Like an art collection, a lava lamp, or a tank of tropical fish, they offer your guests a peripheral sideshow that they can take or leave as they like. With the audio low or muted completely, party videos can also provide guests with a much-needed mental time-out from an evening of social excess: Who better than H. R. Pufnstuf, Rudy Ray Moore, or Liberace to keep you company while you have a quiet smoke, polish off an hors d'oeuvre, or sit catatonically for a few minutes before jumping back into the mix?

For sources, see 📚 by individual title.

Safe and Accessible
Across-the-board amusement.

Hey Folks! It's Intermission Time, *Volume 5*

A+! Five stars! A must! One of the best series of party videos ever! A platinum collection from the lost age of movie theater snack-bar promos and intermission shorts jumps at us through a kaleidoscope of waltzing hot dogs, spinning pizzas, and prancing potato chips, as seen through scratchy stock celluloid dating from the late 1950s to the mid-1970s. We're treated to a full two hours of crude and cool animation, groovy jingles, clock countdowns, and gratuitous soft-drink plugs, with some Cinerama promos, public-service shorts, and small-town regional advertisements thrown in for good measure. There's something about dancing snack-bar imagery that serves a party like no other video can.

Classic Television Commercials, *Volume 4*

Dog food, laundry detergent, hair tonic, cars, and sleeping pills are among the dozens of products represented in this remarkably diverse collection of TV commercials of the '50s, '60s, and '70s. So much more than nostalgia, it is an anthropological trip through the peculiar standards that have shaped American lives since the advent of television. Marvel at some of the dubious and often outrageous methods advertisers used to attempt to sell their products before they resorted to pure sex. Try to wrap your mind around concepts like "air-softening" cigarettes, "modern" soft drinks, and the rough greasy world of "real" men. Ephemeral toys like the Fonz Cycle and the Toni Tennille doll have their place among sugary breakfast foods, Aqua Velva, and Playtex Living Bras. Horrify yourself as you effortlessly sing along to a jingle you haven't heard or even thought about since you were six years old, and marvel at just how dubious those advertising methods were after all.

Monsterama Sci-Fi Late-Night Creature Feature Show

From beyond outer space and beneath the sea lurk the creatures of crude animation that bullets, tanks, grenades, dynamite, and even missiles can't seem to stop. *Attack of the Crab Monster, I Walked with a Zombie, The Mole People, The Giant Mantis, Invaders from Mars, Bela Lugosi Meets a Brooklyn Gorilla*—these were the films that served as a prelude to countless drive-in make-out sessions of the 1950s, and whose coming-attraction trailers and title card imagery makes for peerless party video material today. Over sixty arcane science fiction and monster movies are featured, conveniently boiled down to their most sensational three minutes. An urge for buttered popcorn may ensue.

Campy Classroom Classics

A veritable grab bag from the inimitable genre of motion pictures that only (until now) played the pull-down movie screens of elementary school classrooms. Eight dated masterpieces walk us through such themes as overnight camping trips, the provocative history of canned meats, the dilemmas one might grapple with in a world without paper, the breaking of bad habits, and child abduction defense. Lots of stiff animation, inferior performances, and starched narrative. If played without sound, some of the footage could be passed off as old family home movies (fireside cookouts, small-town carnival rides), until you catch a scene of a happy fourth grader being yanked into a stranger's car on her way home from school. Films include ventriloquist dolls, talking paper bags, and flying hams—this is the apex of educational cinema.

Videos for Altered States
When your mind is a wonderful thing to waste.

H. R. Pufnstuf Live at the Hollywood Bowl
One night Sid and Marty Krofft—creators of some of the most abrasive children's television ever produced (*Bugaloos, Land of the Lost,*

Lidsville, and *Wonderbug,* among others)—commandeered the world-famous Hollywood Bowl and put on a show. It's barely believable that this could have really happened—even in 1973. The evening's bill included H. R. Pufnstuf and his series costar Jack Wild, all six Brady kids, four dwarfs, and *Sigmund and the Sea Monster* star Johnny Whitaker as emcee. SEE Pufnstuf take the stage with an electric guitar and a Mylar wig! WITNESS celebrated midget Billy Barty in drag! HEAR the collective tunelessness of the Brady kids at work, as they simultaneously sing six distinctly different melodies to the same medley of rock 'n' roll oldies! EXPERIENCE the grand finale as an inflatable Pufnstuf pops from a giant cake encircled with assorted Krofft characters riding on toy horses and expands to an intimidating two stories while the American flag is raised over the stage scored by a rousing "Stars and Stripes Forever." *Harsh!* What makes this a perfect party video is that it's much, much better without sound.

Liberace (Boxed set)
That he plays the piano is almost completely incidental: This is the acid test for those who never witnessed Mr. Showmanship in action. Surreal excess and 1970s Las Vegas– style ostentation abound as Liberace vamps across the stage through three mind-bending specials. With his face so taut he looks oddly Asian, Lee (his friends call him Lee) pulls out all the stops: chauffeured onto the stage in a mirrored Rolls Royce, flying over the audience in an ostrich-feather cape, riding a hot-air balloon over the Las Vegas skyline, and tickling the ivories atop a rotating platform set against a backdrop of the "internationally famous dancing waters." Frequent exits "to slip out and get into some-

thing more spectacular" give way to acrobats, variety acts, and gratuitous guests appearances by Vegas standbys Lola Falana, Sandy Duncan, and Phyllis Diller. We're also taken on a tour of Lee's lurid Las Vegas home, including, but certainly not limited to, a moment in the bathtub. The proverbial car wreck!

mescaline. Disturbing subplots underscore the show, as the story unfolds in scenes that take place back at the Brady home. The memory of Mike Brady singing Donna Summer's "Love to Love You Baby" is one your guests won't soon shake off. Painful! With audio, this is like watching eight people being tarred and feathered. Without it, this is a pop-culture circuit blower.

The Brady Bunch Hour, Vol. 1 & 2

First there was *The Brady Bunch*. Then, there was the other *Brady Bunch,* the musical variety show: The Brady Bunch with a low-rent Rockette-style chorus line, a fake Jan, and a new house. In this world where fictions collide, we're reintroduced to an uncomfortably older Brady brood, sporting unfamiliar hairstyles and outfitted with sequined gig wear that actually hurts to look at. They sing, they dance, they perform in comic skits. That part is difficult enough to assimilate. The non sequitur sequences like circus-costumed Bradys frolicking underwater among a bunch of clown-faced firefighters and a hundred helium-filled party balloons is like some Esther Williams number on basement

I Wanna Be a Beauty Queen

Halloween, high fashion, and 1980s decadence share the stage in London's Alternative Miss World pageant, a no-holds-barred beauty contest of the absurd. Contestants like Miss Handled, Miss Winscale Nuclear Disaster, Miss Anthropic, and Miss Piss vie for the coveted title amid a mess of body paint, bubble wrap, false eyelashes, and pyrotechnics. Backstage bustle is interspersed with runway action, and what action it is! Special appearances include Divine as guest emcee and an opening musical sequence performed by the impossibly adorable Little Nell, after which this spectacle is best appreciated without audio.

The Taste Pushers
For guests who are impossible to offend.

Girls Come Too

Its cryptic title speaks more to the era of nude-sploitation films than it does to G-spots. *Girls Come Too* is a foray into the carefree world of clothing-optional recreation from the privileged vantage point of a Miami "naturist" camp, circa 1963. It's the molasses-in-January-paced story of men's magazine pinup Maria Stinger, who travels to Florida on a modeling assignment and finds herself falling for a nudist horse ranch owner. After a little gentle coercion, he serves as her escort to Eden Sunland Paradise, where, it would seem, clothing is optional but two-foot beehive wigs are mandatory. It is here that Maria is tuned in to the kooky (and busy) world of the nudist: weightlifting, shuffleboard, hopscotch, horseshoes, tetherball, baseball, dodgeball (!), croquet, volleyball, gymnastics, jump rope, archery, interpretive modern dance, splashing around in an overcrowded, murky swimming pool, they never stop! The Super 8 epic culminates with the nude wedding of Maria

and her horsey beau. At once compelling and yawn inducing, this second-rate virtual travel tour can't be beat.

Afros, Macks, and Zodiacs: The Best Black Action Films of the '70s

To make the classification "best" in reference to black action movies of the 1970s is redundant, because there is no such thing as a bad black action movie of the '70s. *Afros, Macks, and Zodiacs* presents an unrivaled collection of black action movie trailers, featuring among them *Cleopatra Jones and the Gold Casino, Hell Up in Harlem, Black Caesar, Super Fly*, and *Foxy Brown*. Your guests will reel to the spellbinding *Disco Godfather* and other salient moments from the likes of Pam Grier, Isaac Hayes, Tamara Dobson, and Fred Williamson. The host is Rudy Ray Moore of *Dolemite* and *Monkey Hustle,* who intersperses trailer segments with licentious jokes.

Twisted Sex

From *The Orgy of the Golden Nudes* to *I Was a Man, Twisted Sex* delivers a nonstop ninety-minute spectacular of tawdry coming attractions for the sleaziest, raunchiest, most minimally budgeted sexploitation movies of the 1960s. Don't let the title mislead you, however. This is mid-century sexploitation, after all, where a top-less dry hump is about as X-rated as things ever got. That said, there's still plenty of suggested kink packed into these three-minute teasers, as evidenced by trailers for *Satan's Bed, Ride the Wild Pink Horse,* and *Olga's Massage Parlor.* You might alienate a guest or two, but anyone who fails to see the humor in this collection probably isn't very much fun, anyway.

She-Babes Cavalcade of Sports

Bloody noses, bikinis, backyard catfights, and bare-knockered knockouts—you'll find no corporate sponsors or product endorsement deals among these "athletes." See the premier women of the ring go at it in vintage 1950s black-and-white film shorts. Watch the big bad babes of roller derby give it up on the rink. Bullfighting, pool, fencing, bowling, it's all here, proving that many of the sports typically played by men are no less boring to watch when played by women.

Scene Stealing 4

Intriguing focal points, purposeful amusements, interactive absurdity. The Padophile seizes any opportunity to create a centerpiece that guests can't ignore. Cozying up to a sake table sustaining a garden of living bamboo offers more than a spot to place your cup, and watch how a toilet seat that gives partygoers a creative outlet will keep them coming back for more. These are the elements that provide the Pad partyscape with the distinctions that command attention.

Graffiti-Friendly Toilet Seat

The party doesn't have to stop just because nature calls—a raucous time can be had in the loo by encouraging your guests to sign their work. Boozed up with chalk in hand and locked in the bathroom alone: It's a combination that lends itself well to creative syntax. Capture those inspired moments by turning your toilet seat into a veritable guest book on which friends can doodle, rant, quote, or free-associate. In addition, you'll have your toilet to remind you of a smashing evening long after the last flush.

The chalkboard toilet seat is easy to pull together—all you need is a can of chalkboard paint (sold almost anywhere that has an extensive spray paint selection), fine sandpaper, a toilet seat, and a screwdriver.

Remove the toilet seat lid from its hinges and lightly sand the top surface. Use something like upturned paper cups to prop the toilet seat a few inches above a work surface covered with newspaper. Follow product instructions to spray the chalkboard coating, and allow the surface to dry for at least 24 hours before reattaching to the hinge and inscribing.

Provide guests with a cup filled with colored chalk and a small eraser.

Fireball XL-5 Cocktail Caddy

This caddy is a nod to my friend Dave—a compulsive flea-market shopper—who insists mismatched cocktail glasses are the most efficient way to serve drinks because everyone always knows which glass is theirs. I think this is his way of justifying unnecessary 75¢ purchases, but he has a good point. And with as many years of hard social drinking as he's got under his belt, who am I to argue?

Here, flash follows function. This is a fine way to provide a guest with a glass should they need one, while at the same time providing a showcase for your many mismatched treasures. This glassware stand also serves double duty as a night-light should you happen to pass out before you make it to bed.

Tools

* Clean bucket or large mixing bowl, for mixing the plaster
* 2 stainless steel or plastic mixing bowls, one $8^1/_2$" and one $6^1/_2$", for casting the mold
* Measuring cup
* Medium-grade sandpaper
* Electric drill
* 1" and $^5/_{16}$" drill bits
* Butter knife or slotted screwdriver
* Coping saw, or miter box with saw and cam pins, for cutting the dowels
* Narrow paintbrush, no more than 2" wide
* Newspaper or cardboard
* Disposable plastic container with straight walls and a flat bottom, for mixing the gloss finish
* 2 stirring sticks
* Rubber gloves
* Paper towels

Supplies

* 6 cups dry plaster of paris
* All-purpose glue
* Wooden beads with a $^5/_{16}$" clearance, to top the dowels
* Ten to eighteen $^5/_{16}$" wooden dowels, cut to desired lengths
* Acrylic paint to match the gravel
* 2 pounds aquarium gravel
* EnviroTex Lite Pour-On High Gloss Finish 📖
* 5" watt lamp accessory cord with line switch (photo shows a starlight)
* Decorative appliance bulb
* Felt (optional)

Directions

1. Mix the plaster of paris with 3 cups cold water in the clean bucket or mixing bowl. Stir until smooth and pour into the $8^1/_2$" mixing bowl until the bowl is about two-thirds full. Place the $6^1/_2$" mixing bowl inside the larger bowl, pressing it into the wet plaster, raising the plaster level in the large bowl to its rim (add more wet plaster if necessary). Weight the smaller bowl in place with a measuring cup filled with water until the plaster sets, about 15 minutes.

2. After the plaster has set and dried (12 hours to a couple of days, depending on temperature and humidity), remove the small bowl and tap the hardened plaster form from the large mixing bowl. Sand the edges of the form so they are smooth.

3. Place the form convex-side up on a work surface. Using the 1" bit, drill the placement for the light socket wherever it seems pleasing (see photo; you could also put the light at top center), drilling the hole all the way through. Carve a channel along the underside of the form to allow clearance for ▶

the lamp cord, so that the plaster form can sit flat on a tabletop. (The plaster is very soft and easy to carve—use the butter knife or slotted screwdriver.)

4. Using the $^5/_{16}$" bit, drill the placement of the dowel stems where you'd like them, drilling only 1" or so into the form (see Notes).

5. Glue the wood beads to the tips of the dowels. Set aside to dry (see Notes).

6. Paint the form and when the paint is dry, insert the dowels in place. Use a prop to lift the plaster form so that it is slightly elevated above your work surface (use something like a large, wide roll of duct tape or a small cardboard box). Working on one section at a time, coat the top surface of the form with glue using the 2" paintbrush, avoiding contact with the dowels or the interior of the hole drilled for the bulb.

7. While the glue is still wet, shake the gravel over the applied area, covering it completely. Let dry. Repeat until the entire surface is covered.

8. Clear any loose gravel. With the form propped a couple inches above a wide, heavy layer of newspaper or cardboard, mix the gloss finish according to product instructions with a stirring stick, wearing rubber gloves.

9. Starting at the tip of the dome, carefully pour the finish onto the surface of the gravel, avoiding drizzling over the length of the dowels or pouring into the interior of the hole drilled for the bulb. Pour one section at a time, allowing the liquid to run and coat as much area as possible. The finish should make contact with the point where the dowel meets the gravel. Should you pour any of it into the socket hole, clear it with a stirring stick

before it sets. Once the finish is set in place but still wet, wipe the runoff from the bottom edge with a paper towel.

10. Once dry, sand the bottom edge to remove any dried runoff from the finish. Insert the accessory cord and bulb. Apply felt to the bottom of the form to protect tabletops from any scratches, if you like.

Notes:
Should you make any mistakes in drilling, or should the plaster chip while you're working, you can patch it by mixing more plaster (to a consistency like pancake batter) and applying it by hand onto the trouble spots. Allow it to dry, sand, and continue working.

The dowels may be finished with spray shellac for a deeper color and shine.

Debris **Cage**

At first glance this project may seem only tangentially related to party throwing—if relevant at all—but if you never seem to have enough places to stow the miscellaneous stuff you want out of sight before guests arrive, take note. In my home these are invaluable. They're an efficient and cheap way to stash magazines, dog toys, half-finished art projects, and anything else you want out of the way by party time.

Tools

* Scissors or paper cutter
* Pencil
* Utility knife
* Metal ruler
* Hot-glue gun and glue sticks
* Miter box with saw and cam pins
* Sheet metal shears
* Mixing bowl
* Fork

Supplies

* Foreign newspaper
* $1/4$" two-ply cardboard (the heavy cardboard from moving boxes used for packing dishes and other fragile items)
* $3/4$" x $3/4$" oak corner guard (see Notes)
* Wood glue
* 23-gauge $1/4$" hardware cloth (see Notes)
* $1^{1}/_{2}$ cups all-purpose flour
* 1 cup hot water

Directions

1. Cut the choicest pieces of newspaper into a variety of $1/2$" to 3" strips, up to lengths of 7".

2. The measurements of the cage can be designed to your specifications, depending on what you need to house, but this container is designed to measure 11" x $12^{1}/_{2}$" x 4" high. Using the utility knife and metal ruler, and cutting square with the grain of the cardboard, cut a bottom piece measuring $10^{1}/_{2}$" x 12". Next cut the 4 side pieces: 2 measuring 4" x 12", and 2 measuring 4" x 11".

3. Run a line of hot glue along one 12" cut edge of the bottom panel. Attach a 12" side panel against the cut edge of the bottom panel. Repeat with the opposite side panel.

4. Run a line of hot glue along the cut U-shaped face edges of the construction and apply the 11" end panel flush against it. Repeat with the opposite end panel.

5. Using the miter box, cut four pieces of the oak corner guard: 2 pieces measuring $13^{1}/_{8}$" at their ►

longest points, and 2 pieces measuring 11⁶/₈" at their longest points. Using the wood glue (or a very fine layer of hot glue) applied between the cut angled edges of the corner guards, join the pieces together to create the framework for the box top.

6. With the sheet metal shears, cut a sheet of hardware cloth 11" x 12¹/₂". Manipulate it so that it's completely flat. Press it under a weight if necessary.

7. Mix the flour and hot water in the mixing bowl, and stir quickly with a fork to break up any clumping in the flour. Add a good squirt or two of the wood glue to the mix and stir well (see Notes).

8. One at a time, dip the wider-strips of newspaper into the flour mix, drag both sides across the lip of the mixing bowl to remove excess liquid, and adhere to the cardboard bin. Create a patchwork of text, being mindful of the distribution of large bold text and small print, completely covering the visible surface of the cardboard. Repeat the process with the famework for the lid using the small strips of newspaper carefully pressing and tucking the edges under the lip of the corner guard to keep the lines sharp. To dry, stand the pieces on upturned drinking glasses to keep the wet paper from making contact with your work surface.

9. Once all the pieces are bone dry, gently press the panel of wire mesh into the framework of the lid. It should fit snugly without buckling. Working in 4" or 5" sections, run a thin line of hot glue where the edge of the wire meets the inside corner of the framework. Lightly hold the wire in place until the glue sets. Continue until the entire edge of the wire panel is glued into place. Let the glue set and cool before applying the lid.

Notes:
Hardware cloth is a galvanized wire mesh similar to chicken wire. It can be found in the garden section of most hardware stores.

Oak corner guard is a finishing trim used in cabinetmaking and other building projects. It is sold in lumber yards and large hardware stores, usually along-side base-board trim and decorative molding.

The flour and water should have a grainy consistency, giving the finished surface texture and a roughly hewn look to the overall product. If you're aiming for a smoother surface, add more water and more glue, and whisk the mixture to the consistency of whole milk.

Bamboo Garden *Sake Table*

Whether your guests are sake drinkers or not, they'll surely appreciate the opportunity to kick their shoes off, sprawl out, and lounge around this tabletop grouping of living bamboo that rises a mere 10½" off the floor. Great for sipping tea around to come down from an evening, this table works nicely both indoors and out.

Tools

* Pencil
* Ruler
* 2 chairs or small boxes, to prop up the tabletop while drilling and cutting
* Electric drill
* ³/₈" and ⁵/₃₂" drill bits
* Jigsaw
* Miter box with saw and cam pins
* Medium- to fine-grade sandpaper
* Newspaper
* Hammer
* Level

Supplies

* 3 matching bowls of varying sizes (see Notes)
* 2' x 4' sheet of ³/₄" medium density fiberboard (MDF) for the tabletop
* Paint, varnish, or tung oil
* 15' length of 1" diameter split rattan pole
* Spray shellac
* Wood glue
* ⁵/₈" x 19 wire brads

* One 5' foot pole of 3" diameter bamboo
* Eight ½" corner braces with screws
* Gravel or small pebbles to fill the bowls (see Notes) Several stalks of sprouted bamboo (see Notes)

Directions

1. With the bowls placed upside down on the tabletop, determine the spots you'd like them positioned (see Notes). Using the pencil, trace the rim of each bowl. Remove the bowl and measure the edge of its lip. If the bowls have a lip measuring ¼", for instance, draw another circle centered inside each traced circle ¼" smaller in circumference, using the outside line as your guide. The pencil line does not need to be a perfect, it only needs to provide a line for you to follow with the jigsaw.

2. Prop up the tabletop and, using the ³/₈" bit, drill a hole just inside the line of the smaller cir-cle. Slip the blade of the jigsaw into the hole and saw, following the line of the smaller circle and cutting a hole in which to sink the bowl. The bowl should fit inside the cut hole resting on its rim, with its lip concealing the edge of the hole. Repeat for the remaining two bowls. Clear the tabletop of dust, and paint or finish.

3. Measure the split rattan and cut the ends at 45° angles in the miter box. You'll need 2 pieces measuring 25" at their longest points, and 2 pieces measuring 49" at their longest points.

4. Sand the ends of the cut rattan, place on newspaper, flat-side down, and spray with shellac. Use 2 or 3 coats, allowing each coat to dry completely before applying the next (about 10 minutes).

5. Once the shellac is completely dry, tap a finishing nail into each end of one 49" piece of rattan, about 1½" from the end, driving ▶

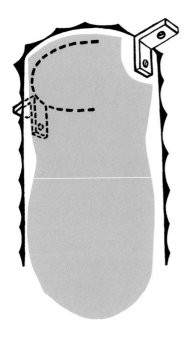

the nail only deep enough to stay anchored. Prop the tabletop securely on the floor. Smear a line of wood glue along the 4' edge of the tabletop. Position the rattan rim so the top of the trim is flush with the tabletop, and hammer into place. Add additional finishing nails evenly spaced at 9" points from the two initial nails, to secure the trim. Complete with the remaining 3 sides (on the 2' sides of the table, finishing nails should be spaced evenly at 7" points from the initial nails.

6. Cut 4 pieces of the bamboo pole into 10" lengths (see Note,

page 15), then sand the edges. Determine which direction you'd like each bamboo section positioned when attached to the tabletop.

7. Attach a corner brace on each side of the top edge of the bamboo leg, flush with its rim. Do this by standing the bamboo top-side down on a work surface, positioning the corner braces against the bamboo, and marking their screw holes with the pencil. Remove the braces, drill leads on the pencil marks with the $^5/_{32}$" bit, then attach the corner braces with screws. Repeat with the remaining 3 legs.

8. Flip the tabletop upside down and position each bamboo leg 2" from the edge of each corner. Mark the screw holes of the corner braces with the pencil, remove the legs, and drill leads. Reposition the legs and secure into place with the screws. Use the level to ensure an even tabletop.

Notes:

The bowls holding the bamboo stalks—mixing bowls were used here—look best if they have a lip large enough to conceal the edge of the hole cut into the surface of the tabletop. When choosing placement for the bowls,

keep in mind that the bowls should sit at least 3" from the edge of the tabletop: there must be enough room to allow for the bamboo legs and their hardware.

Sprouted bamboo can be found year-round in many nurseries, florists, and Asian gift shops, planted in gravel or pebbles. All the bamboo needs to thrive is a stationary position in the gravel (burying the bottom 2" or more of the stem), a little sunlight, and enough water to rise to the surface of the gravel.

You may find that due to irregularities in the bamboo, the tabletop may not be completely level once the legs have been attached. If you need to reduce a particular leg, simply remove it and sand the foot of the leg to remove the necessary portion. If you're using an electric sander, use a medium to fine paper and be aware that the bamboo fiber will respond quickly, creating the risk of oversanding. If you need to add height to a particular leg, remove the leg and slip a thin nylon washer or two over one or both screws, positioned between the corner brace and the underside of the table, and reattach the leg.

The **Traction** Ashtray

The original hanging ashtray experienced its big heyday in the late 1950s and early 1960s, offered by mail-order companies as a stylish way for party-minded smokers to "free up tabletop space." For one reason or another, the trend never quite caught on. In an effort to bring back the craze that never was, here's your step-by-step guide to the hanging ashtray of the twenty-first century: a sculptural amusement cut with a dash of architectural engineering. This surreal accessory will allow guests to extinguish their cigarettes in suspended style, and its inviting curves will have even those with virgin lungs lighting up for the opportunity to sample its charms.

Disclaimer: This project is labor intensive, but great fun for the truest of DIY spirits. It also allows considerable room for interpretation.

Tools

* Yardstick
* Sheet metal shears
* Bucket
* Scissors
* Large bowl of cold water
* 2 paintbrushes
* Superfine-grade sandpaper
* Wooden spoon or stirring stick
* Electric drill
* $3/16$" and $9/64$" drill bits
* Cable cutters
* Hammer

Supplies

* 24" x 24" piece of 23-gauge $1/4$" hardware cloth (see Note, page 126)
* 1 roll plaster cloth
* 4 cups dry plaster of paris
* 1" diameter wood dowel, cut to a length of 20"
* $1/16$" galvanized aircraft cable (see Note)

* Six $1/16$" cable ferrules
* Three $5/32$" x $1^5/8$" eye bolts, each with 2 nuts
* Six #8 washers
* Ceiling hook
* Sand or gravel as needed

Directions

1. Create the wire form by cutting a piece of hardware cloth to the dimensions illustrated. Pull the bottom-right corner of the piece to meet a point about 9" from the right corner of the top edge, creating a wide cone. Secure by folding over the hardware cloth along the dotted line, as shown. Gently shape the form to create a smooth cavity and a sweeping flat edge.

2. Work over a surface that resists water. Use a bucket to hold the form in place while you work on the plastering. Cut the plaster ▶

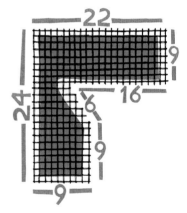

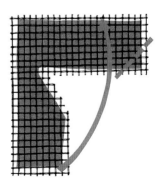

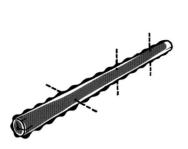

cloth into strips about 4" wide. Dip individual strips into the cold water, apply the strip to the wire form much like you'd use papier-mâché, and then smooth the strip into place with a wet paintbrush. Work in sections until the entire form is covered. Mask the entire form with a total of 4 or 5 layers of plaster cloth, allowing each layer to dry completely before applying the next, paying particular attention to covering the sharp edges and corners of the form.

3. Once the form is covered and the plaster cloth has completely hardened, lightly sand rough areas for a smooth finish.

4. Mix 2 parts plaster of paris to 1 part cold water and stir until smooth. Using a paintbrush, coat the surface of the form with wet plaster, spreading it as evenly as possible. Once hardened, mix more plaster and coat the reverse side. Allow to dry completely, ideally overnight. Sand the surface of the form smooth. If necessary, apply more wet plaster to mask rough spots or to smooth lines.

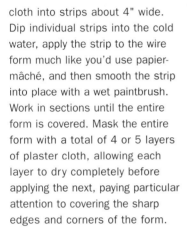

5. Using the $^3/_{16}$" bit, drill holes for the eye bolts. Space 2 holes, about $3^1/_2$" apart, at a spot about $3^1/_2$" from the narrow, triangular point of the form. Drill another hole at a spot about $1^1/_2$" from the front angled, wide edge of the form. Positioning for the eye bolts can be approximate, because each form will have a slightly different shape and weight.

6. With the $^9/_{64}$" bit, drill 3 holes through the dowel, 2 placed 4" from each end, and 1 center, positioned as shown.

7. Cut 2 pieces of cable, 1 measuring 20" and 1 measuring 9". Slip the 20" cable through the horizontally positioned end hole.

8. Slide a cable ferrule over each end of the cable. Loop the end of each cable through an eye bolt, then slide the end of the cable back through the ferrule. Place the ferrule flat onto a hard work surface and give it one good slam with the hammer to secure the cables into the ferrule channels.

9. Secure the 9" cable through the hole at the opposite end of the dowel, using 2 cable ferrules, as previously done.

10. Secure the center ceiling suspension cable, cut to your desired length, using one cable ferrule to secure the cable to the dowel, and another to create a top loop from which to hang the final assembly.

11. Thread each eye bolt first with a hex nut, then a washer, and place them into the holes drilled for them in the plaster shell. From the underside of the form, slip another washer and hex nut onto each eye bolt and gently tighten.

12. Hang the assembly and fill the cavity of the form with the sand or gravel.

Note:

You will need enough cable to cut one 20" length and one 9" length, plus the length you determine for the height from which the form will be hung.

52 Pickup Table Runner

Put your cards on the table with a harmlessly naughty runner fashioned from 2 decks—that's 100 beauties, not counting the jokers—of nudie playing cards. That's a whole lotta feminine (or masculine, if you like) pulchritude gracing one buffet. A runner like this one really doesn't serve any important purpose except to provide hungry guests with a tabletop skin show, but if you are looking to dress up a buffet without fussy linens, here's your answer. Depending on the size of the cards being used, this will make a runner measuring approximately 14" x 48".

Tools

* Hole punch
* Ballpoint pen
* Scissors

Supplies

* 2 decks of girlie (or manly) playing cards
* 15 yards of $1/4$" flat ribbon
* Tape

Directions

1. Using a joker, create a template for the hole placement by folding the card in half lengthwise and pressing the crease sharply. Unfold the card, then fold it in half again, this time across the width, again pressing the crease. Unfold the card. The creases will serve as the perfect center points to guide the hole punch.

2. Punch a hole centered at each crease, $1/8$" from each edge of the card. This will serve as your template.

3. Place your template over the backside of each playing card and trace the inside of each hole with a ballpoint pen onto the card underneath.

4. Punch each hole on the marks.

5. Working with the cards face down, weave them together with the ribbon lengthwise first, creating 6 rows of cards, each 14 cards long. You will cut the ribbon at the end of each row. After they've been woven into place (see illustration), adjust the cards so that they lie with their edges barely touching. Fold each end of loose ribbon back onto the end card and tape securely in place.

6. Connect the individually woven rows by weaving them together side-by-side, working with the cards face down. Adjust the cards as before, with edges barely touching, folding and taping the loose ends of the ribbon.

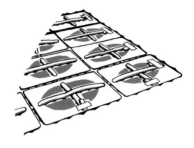

Beaded Hors d'Oeuvre Spears

For an hors d'oeuvre spear more substantial than a toothpick but simpler than a cocktail fork, festoon plain bamboo skewers with wood or glass beads. A waterproof finish makes these spears washable and reusable. The beads should fit snugly enough when strung over the bamboo to hold their place. It's necessary that you bring a plain skewer with you when selecting beads to use in this project, as many beads are drilled irregularly and each bead should first be tested over the skewer to ensure a proper fit.

Tools

* Kitchen scissors or gardening shears
* Fine-grade sandpaper
* Disposable plastic cup
* Stirring stick
* 2 small disposable paintbrushes
* Small block of styrofoam (like a piece used to pack electronics) or florist foam
* One 4" x 11" piece of poster board, folded in half, notches cut along the top of the fold

Supplies

* Bamboo skewers (sold in the cooking supplies section in supermarkets)
* Beads
* Envirotex Lite Pour-On High Gloss Finish 📓

Directions

1. Cut each bamboo skewer to a length of 4" with a pair of kitchen scissors or gardening shears. Smooth the cut end with fine sandpaper to remove splintering, with single strokes toward the snipped end to keep the bamboo from splintering further.

2. String the beads to the cut end of the skewer, so that they are held snugly in place.

3. In a well-ventilated, dust-free area, mix a cupful of high-gloss finish following product instructions. Completely submerge the beaded end of the skewer into the cup filled with the finish, dipping no more than half the length of the skewer.

4. As soon as you pull the skewer from the finish, use a paintbrush to remove excess liquid, being careful to leave enough to allow for a complete seal. Stab the pick into the styrofoam and leave to dry completely.

5. Mix another cupful of finish, and dip the opposite end of each skewer, as before. Brush away excess finish. Lean each skewer on its side over the folded piece of poster board in a notch to prevent its rolling or touching another skewer while it dries. Be sure that absolutely nothing touches the wet end. Allow to dry and cure completely, about 36 hours.

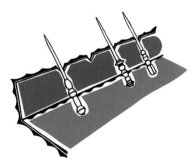

Gifted

5

For the DIY set, the offering of a gift is never a perfunctory occasion. It's an opportunity to work their creative juices into a lather, to think outside the gift box, and to produce something tailored to the inclinations, obsessions, or idiosyncratic bent of the recipient. But a handmade gift isn't simply a finished product, it's a gesture that speaks to the thought and attention required to create it. Not every party is a gift-giving event, but for the ones that are, it's always inspiring to consider options of the hand-rendered variety, particularly when it comes to reinventing the flotsam of the twentieth century. If you have a selective eye and a little inspiration, postconsumer products can serve as guideposts to the perfect gift.

33⅓ Popcorn Bowl

Speak to anyone who remembers buying music pre–compact disc, and they will undoubtedly wax nostalgic about vinyl. Fumbling with the hologram security stickers and plastic casing of a new CD just can't compete with the inimitable experience of cracking open and peeling away the shrink-wrap cellophane sealing a new record (so alive with static electricity that it would shift and cling to your forearm or thigh) and getting that first whiff of the ambrosial off-gassing from the freshly pressed vinyl disc inside. With the purchase of each LP came this cherished mini-event redolent of promise, the sweet bouquet of new music, bad for the brain perhaps, but good for the soul.

While there is certainly no turning back—and we might someday even find ourselves waxing poetic over breaking the security seals on CDs—there's still reason to get excited around the scent of vinyl with the 33⅓ Popcorn Bowl.

Tools
* Kitchen oven
* 6" terra-cotta flowerpot
* Oven mitts

Supplies
* Full-length vinyl LP

Directions

1. Position rack low in the oven to provide plenty of clearance for the flowerpot. Preheat to 400°F.

2. If your record needs cleaning, wipe it with a damp towel. Center the record on top of the upside-down flowerpot and place it on the center of the rack.

3. Bake for 1 minute or less, checking progress often, until the record has gone limp and hangs loosely over the flower pot.

4. Using oven mitts and touching only the bottom rim of the flower pot, remove from the oven—being careful not to disturb the record—and place on a heat-resistant surface to cool.

5. You can further shape the sides of the vinyl bowl to your satisfaction just after you've pulled it from the oven, while it is still pliable. If you want a different shape, experiment with any oven-safe bowl or pot: mixing bowls, oversized soup bowls, saucepans, and the like. As soon as it's out of the oven, try sandwiching the record between two bowls or flowerpots to give the shape more height or a tighter edge. Once cooled, the bowl can be washed with warm soapy water. Do not place in the dishwasher.

Out of **the Box**

Who says a gift needs to be wrapped in a box? Who says a gift needs to be wrapped at all?

Any gift is more intriguing when presented in one of these cryptic containers, fashioned simply from 1-quart paint cans (available new in the paint department of any hardware store) and mail-order ad clippings from the back pages of old magazines good for nothing else. Since the cans seal airtight, they make great containers for perishable edible gifts and for items like coffee beans, expensive tea, or incense. Add some shredded paper, and they're a safe way to package small breakables like holiday ornaments.

The greatest advantage to this no-wrap wrap, however, is that this packaging will almost certainly enjoy a second life as a pencil cup, stash can, catchall for the dresser or worktable, or may even serve to actually contain paint.

Sloppy One-Night-Stand Preparedness Kit

This is one gift that keeps on giving, in a manner of speaking, inspired by a good friend known to make frequent trips to Rome, Amsterdam, Copenhagen, Montreal, New York, and Boston, never failing to return from his travels with yet another notch on his well-worn belt. Since he lives simply but furnishes his life with the finest of everything, he falls into the "hard to buy for" category come gift time.

This is a one-size-fits-all solution for the indiscriminate of either sex. It is a sexual "survival kit" housed in a capped shipping tube, cut to size with a miter box and a coping saw with a superfine blade. Because the tube was made to protect materials that can't be folded or creased, the casing is quite durable and may be confidently tossed into soft luggage, the trunk of a car, a backpack, or the saddlebag of your hog without the risk of being crushed. The container is discreet enough so that it won't raise an eyebrow (Blueprints? Tinker Toys? Flares for the car perhaps?) or sound an alarm at check-in, and depending on predilection, the contents can be tailored to suit a variety of players.

78-RPM Photo Album

I'm a sucker for good cover art. Not only is a multi-sleeved 78-RPM album (the origin of our still-general usage of the term) necessary for this project, these often sport great cover art. So if I find myself in a junk shop or flea market digging through a bin of old 78s, I will inevitably come home with something that I didn't have enough self-restraint to leave behind. The music is often negligible, or missing entirely, or I'll find that a Tchaikovsky record has been mistakenly slipped into the sleeve of a Desi Arnaz cover long ago, leaving each incomplete.

But there's no need for this great cover art to go unappreciated, disintegrating in dusty thrift shop bins or rotting in damp basements at the tenacious hands of merciless fungi. A little reinvention can easily transform an item that has lost its purpose into an inspired gift.

Tools

* X-acto knife
* Yardstick
* Paper cutter or scissors
* Spray-mount adhesive
* Electric drill
* $7/32$" drill bit
* Ruler
* Pencil or ballpoint pen
* Slotted screwdriver

Supplies

* 1 favorite 78-RPM hardbound album with multiple sleeves, 12" x 10$1/4$" (standard measurement for 78s)
* 4 to 8 sheets of 19$1/2$" x 25$1/2$" watercolor paper
* $8/32$" x $1/2$" aluminum binding posts and screws

Directions

1. Using the X-acto knife, slice away the inner sleeves bound inside the album cover, cutting along the inside crease where the sleeves meet the spine. You should be left with only the hard cover and a clean inner spine.

2. Trim a piece of the watercolor paper to 10" x 24". Place the album cover open flat on your work surface and brush away any debris. Spray one side of the watercolor paper with spray-mount adhesive. Place the sheet over the existing inner liner and spine of the album, adhesive-side down. Press out any air pockets.

3. Flip the album over. Mark a spot 2" from the top edge of the spine and 2" from the bottom edge of the spine, centered. This is where you'll insert the screws to bind your pages. With the $7/32$" drill bit, drill a hole through the spine (and the new inner lining) on those marks. ▶

4. Cut each remaining full sheet of watercolor paper in half lengthwise, to create 2 sheets measuring 9$^3/_4$" x 25$^1/_2$". So that the sheets fit into the album without any overhang, trim an additional 2" off the length of each sheet, for a final measurement of 9$^3/_4$" x 23$^1/_2$".

5. Flip the album back over so that it's open and flat. Position a trimmed sheet of watercolor paper inside the album as it would be bound and, using the ruler as your guide, make vertical folds in the paper to match the creases in the spine. Matching the placement of the drilled holes, puncture each sheet with the end of a pencil or ballpoint pen. Repeat with the remaining sheets.

6. Stack the sheets together, flat, on top of the open cover, with all the punctured holes aligned perfectly with the holes in the spine. Place a binding post in each set of holes, pushing through every sheet of paper and into the spine. Working from the flip side, insert the screws into each binding post and tighten with the screwdriver.

Wrapper's Delight

Considering the going price per sheet, the amount of paper usually wasted by miscalculation, and the leftover pieces that will get stashed in a closet, creased and rendered useless, there may be a more efficient approach to the matter of wrapping gifts than commercial wrapping paper.

When the gift in question is of modest size and you want to get it done quickly using what you've got at hand, throw your favorite shirt on the scanner and print yourself up a custom sheet of gift paper in minutes. All you really need to wrap things up is a paper shopping bag, a great wardrobe, and that requisite household appliance, the personal computer.

These wrapping papers were made from clothing pressed onto a scanner and printed onto pieces of shopping bags cut to 8$^1/_2$" x 11". Any paper substantial enough to hold the ink and run smoothly through your printer will do. You can store your scans to use at a future time and you have the extra bonus of being able to arrive at a party dressed to match your gift, should you be the type to do such a thing.

RE/SEARCH #10:
INCREDIBLY STRANGE FILMS
RE/SEARCH #14: Incredibly Strange Music
googie fifties coffee shop architecture
LEGENDS, LIES & Cherished Myths of American History
ALEX DE JONGE
THE LIFE AND TIMES OF
THE WILD WILD WORLD OF THE CRAMPS
FOREVER BARBIE
M. G. LORD
MORROW
AUDI
TECHNOPOLY
Neil Postman
LIDDY
WILL
BY GEORGE
A KAUFMAN COLLECTION
NAGEL'S
EGYPT
MODERN LIBRARY
ERIC STANTON
HARPO SPEAKS!
Neil Postman
AMUSING
ROALD DAHL
Kiss

Eyeglass
Photo Frames

You don't have to look too far or too hard to find a good gift. Everyone has a spare set of sunglass or eyeglass frames lying around somewhere, missing a lens, in need of a tiny screw, or missing one wing. Often a great pair of vintage frames with Coke-bottle lenses are picked up cheaply in a thrift store, slated to be re-lensed for sunglasses or a personal prescription at some undetermined future time that never comes. Undeniably, some are small pieces of art, too great to toss out but not practical enough or sized appropriately to wear. This is a great way to preserve the artistic integrity of those little gems and put them to use.

Pictures printed on better-quality photo paper work best in the frames because they resist buckling. Working from the backside of the frames, trace directly onto the front of the photo with a fine-pointed pen. When cutting the tracing, cut just outside the traced line; this will allow for further trimming to get the best fit. Once you've cut a photo too small to fit the frame, it won't work. It's also important to be aware that the outlines for the photos are traced from the backside of the frames, resulting in each photo fitting the lens opening opposite from the one in which it was traced.

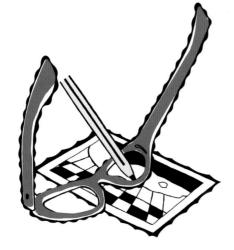

The Gift of **Voodoo**

Everyone loves a good voodoo doll. It's an unconventional all-purpose gift.

The practice of voodoo in the United States is an unlikely patchwork of traditions. What started as the folk religion of Haiti became embellished with Roman Catholic beliefs from the French Colonial period of the 1700s, and then cross-pollinated with the African magical elements and rituals practiced by slaves of Dahomeyan origin. Fast forward to the bustle of the old New Orleans French Quarter and an infamous character like Marie Laveau, and voodoo changes shape once again, becoming an American novelty and a common pop-culture reference, showing up in drive-in horror films, rockabilly tunes, the odd cocktail bar interior, and a memorable episode of *Gilligan's Island*.

While the paraphernalia of voodooists varies, the definitive symbol across the realm of voodoo is the classic voodoo doll itself: darkly mysterious, exotic, foreboding. The most fun in making a voodoo doll for a gift is that the materials you use can be riddled with personal meaning. Fabric torn from a noteworthy article of clothing, dried grasses pulled from the side of a headstone, and beads, a lock of hair, or other embellishments culled from significant sources all contribute to a voodoo doll that is custom tailored to suit the inclinations and idiosyncrasies of its recipient. Keep in mind that the cutting, stitching, and sculpting required here can be roughly crafted. In fact, the most convincing voodoo dolls are the ones crudest in form.

Tools

* Ruler
* Scissors
* Sewing needle

Supplies

* 2 relatively straight twigs or dowels, about 3/8" in diameter, one 15" and one 7"
* Twine
* Wood glue
* 2 chicken bones, ideally drum-sticks, cleaned and dried (see Note)
* Two 8-ounce bags dry Spanish moss 📄

* One 500-yard spool black cotton thread (mercerized cotton-covered polyester)
* Cloth measuring 8" x 18"
* Beads and other embellish-ments, for detail

Directions

1. Make a cross with the 2 twigs at a point about 4" from the end of the long piece and fasten the junction securely with twine. Once tied, add wood glue to the cross point. Let dry.

2. Position a chicken bone at the end of each shorter twig, so that the end of the bone and the end of the twig overlap about 1". Secure with twine and wood glue. Let dry.

3. Form patches of the moss around the wooden framework, creating the body of the doll. Secure the moss in place by winding it with thread and tying securely. Continue to pack the form with more moss, working up to the shoulders and over the fastened ends of the chicken bones a little at a time, winding and securing with thread as you work. ▶

4. Pack the neck of the form, padding the frame and securing the moss in place with thread.

5. Trim the cloth to the pattern shown and slip the center hole of the cloth over the neck of the form. With the length of the cloth lying over the front and back of the form, stitch the side seams together.

6. Tie a thread tightly around the base of the neck. Shape a handful of moss over the neck of the form to finish the head. Wind the thread snugly up the neck over the loose moss, and over the form of the head. Wind the thread tightly to prevent unraveling. Tie securely.

7. Use beads to add eyes, stitching them into place. Use strung beads, bones, stones, charms, and other trimming to finish decorating the doll.

Note:
Drumstick bones work best for the arms. Remove as much of the chicken as possible from the bones, then boil them in plain water until any remaining meat or cartilage falls off easily. Scrub the bones clean, dry them, and let them sit—preferably in the sun or a sunny windowsill—until completely dry.

Mauna Loa Incense Burner

If you've always wanted to try your hand at sculpture but lack the talent of a Michelangelo, Rodin, or even a Brancusi, whet your chisel with the Mauna Loa Incense Burner. Starting from a simple plaster cast and using little more than a screwdriver and a piece of sandpaper, you can create a purposeful component to an engaging party atmosphere, or make a great gift for a friend who longs for a life where the palm trees sway. The plaster is soft, forgiving, and very easy to sculpt. The form is simple and virtually foolproof: Anyone can carve a convincing volcano. Your work may not end up behind glass at Saint Peter's basilica, but you're sure to receive rave reviews from the casual observer.

Tools

* Heavy plastic bag, like the kind used for potting soil
* Duct tape
* Mixing bucket, for plaster
* Stirring stick
* Rope or heavy twine
* Handsaw
* Electric drill
* $1^{1}/_{2}$" drill bit
* Screwdrivers of varying sizes
* Rough- and fine-grade sandpaper
* Clean, dry paint brush
* Bowl or plate, to mix paint
* Medium and fine artist paint-brushes
* Paper towels or napkins

Supplies

* $4^{1}/_{2}$-pound carton plaster of paris
* Photo of a volcano
* Acrylic paint in black, red, and orange
* Clear acrylic spray finish
* Incense cone

Directions

1. Starting from one of the bottom corners, fold the plastic bag into a triangle and tape the seam with bands of duct tape torn lengthwise in half and wrapped around the circumference of the bag. Size the funnel approximately 12" long and 8" wide.

2. Mix 2 parts plaster to 1 part water and pour enough into the plastic bag to create an inverted cone casting. Tie the open end of the bag off with a piece of rope or twine.

3. Secure a good spot to hang the bag while the plaster hardens; from the center rung of a ladder, a rafter in the garage, the top track of a sliding shower door, or any-place it can hang off the ground, undisturbed. Tie and hang the bag securely.

4. Once the plaster has hardened and cooled, remove the plastic and let the casting sit in an arid, well-ventilated area until completely dry. This could take one to several days, depending on the size of the cast and the moisture in the air (see Notes).

5. The sharp-pointed end of the casting will serve as the volcano's tip. Use the hand saw to slice a flat base for the bottom of your sculpture, so that the pointed tip stands straight when placed on a tabletop.

6. To drill the crater, saw the tip of the sculpture flat to create an area about 2" in diameter. Using the $1^{1}/_{2}$" drill bit, make a hole about 1" deep.

7. Using the volcano photo as your guide, dig at the plaster with the screwdrivers to sculpt a surface ▶

of clefts and fissures streaming from the crater. Use the sandpapers to smooth edges and create texture.

8. Once completed, clean with the dry paintbrush to remove as much of the plaster dust as possible.

9. To finish, mix some black acrylic paint with water until it's thin enough to drip from the end of a brush. Working in sections, brush some paint onto the plaster and immediately wipe down with a paper towel. If you think the finish is too light, paint and wipe the surface again. Repeat as necessary. Do not paint inside the crater.

10. Water down and mix some red paint until it drips from the end of a brush. Starting at the top of the volcano, let one drop of paint fall into the top of a crevice and let the paint run down its channel (see Notes). Repeat with the remaining channels at the mouth of the volcano. Next, paint the inside walls of the crater.

11. Once dry, repeat the process over the existing stripes of red paint, this time using orange.

12. When the paint is completely dry, treat the entire form with 1 or 2 coats of clear acrylic spray finish. Place the incense cone in the crater.

Note:
The casting is dry enough to start carving as soon as it's hardened. However, wait until the form is *completely* dry before sanding.

Experiment with different utensils and tools to scrape and carve the plaster—a dinner fork, an ice pick, an awl. If you find that you've scraped too much plaster away or want to build up a particular area, mix more plaster and, just as it starts to thicken, drizzle over the desired area. Allow to dry completely before you resume working, 30 minutes to a couple of hours, depending on the amount.

While painting, if you're not happy with a particular result, immediately dampen a paper towel and wipe off what you've done. Watered-down acrylic is easy to remove if you catch it in time, and easy to mask if you don't.

Dioramic Table Lighter

Back in the day when smoking was PC, the table lighter was as common to living room accoutrements as the toaster was to the kitchen, gracing the tops of home bars and coffee tables anywhere you were apt to find a martini glass. Their popularity peaked about the same time the country became sexually liberated; slowly but surely, they've been all but eliminated from the American partyscape altogether.

For a lighter with a future, you can cast your very own, embedded with virtually anything you can hold in the palm of your hand. As long as you're able to withstand the magnitude of the fumes produced by the styrene and polyester resin, the possibilities are endless.

Tools

* Latex gloves
* Painter's face mask, for protection from the fumes
* 3 or more mixing cups (like disposable plastic party cups) 📓
* 3 or more stirring sticks
* Clean plastic container for casting (an 8-ounce plastic sour cream container was used for the project shown here)
* Electric drill
* 1$^1/_2$" drill bit
* Soft paintbrush and soft dusting cloth
* Fine-grade sandpaper
* Newspaper

Supplies

* 16-ounce can Castin'Craft Polyester Resin 📓
* 1-ounce bottle catalyst for polyester resin
* Items for embedding
* High-gloss resin spray
* 1$^1/_2$" diameter table lighter insert 📓

Directions

1. For best results, cast the mold upside down; the bottom of the container will be the top of the lighter. Wearing latex gloves and a face mask, mix the resin per product instructions. Pour a $^3/_4$" layer at the bottom of the container. Do not embed into this layer—this will be the section of the lighter that holds the hardware.

2. Once the layer has gelled (20 to 30 minutes), mix another batch of resin. You may want to start the embedding process with this second layer. You should need no more than a total of 4 layers for the project—allow each layer to gel before pouring the next.

3. After the mold has set (allow 24 hours), release it from the mold. With the 1$^1/_2$" bit, drill a hole $^3/_4$" deep into the top center of the casting.

4. Brush the casting clear of dust using a soft paintbrush and dusting cloth, being careful not to scratch the surface of the resin. If the bottom edge of the casting is rough, gently sand it smooth.

5. With the casting placed on sheets of newspaper, coat its surface with high-gloss spray (you may want to prop the casting on the cap of the spray can to keep it from sticking to the newspaper).

6. Once completely dry, insert the lighter hardware.

Note:

When using resin products, work in an extremely well-ventilated area free of dust.

📓 Note **Pad**

Retailers, catalog, and source information

Abaca matting. One of many tropical mattings and Polynesian/Hawaiian building materials available through Oceanic Arts. *See* Oceanic Arts for catalog and ordering info.

Adult Contact Publications, many of which are published by East West Publications, are usually sold at adult sex-theme stores. You can also order one of East West's many specialized titles by phone, at (401) 453-5306.

Afros, Macks, and Zodiacs: The Best Black Action Films of the '70s. *See* Something Weird Video for catalog info.

Asian Takeaways. *See* Normal Records.

Bamboo poles. A selection of bamboo and reed materials is available through Oceanic Arts. Poles may be purchased singly or in bales, and can be cut or split to order for a nominal charge. *See* Oceanic Arts.

Beat at Cinecittà. *See* Crippled Dick Hot Wax.

Betty Page Danger Girl: Burlesque Music. *See* QDK Media.

The Brady Bunch Hour, **Volumes 1 & 2.** *See* Rhino. For more on the the sick, sick, world of *The Brady Bunch Hour,* visit www.bradyhour.com.

Campy Classroom Classics. Volume 1 in this four-volume series includes shorts on germs, teeth, manners, skin care, baby-sitting, safety patrol, poison, strangers, and courtesy. *See* Something Weird Video for catalog info.

Castin'Craft Polyester Resin. For a complete listing of polyester resin products, accessories, and retailers, visit www.eti-usa.com or call (707) 443-9323 for product information.

Circus of Life and *The Essential Perrey & Kingsley* are both available through RE/search, the publishers responsible for the celebrated subculture book *Incredibly Strange Films,* among others. An especially noteworthy title in the RE/search collection is their book *Incredibly Strange Music,* which coined the term that created a category of sound theretofore unclassified and which served as an important forerunner to the resurgence in lounge and exotica; a must for the audiophile dancing on the edge. CDs and publications are available at www.researchpubs.com.

Classic Television Commercials, **Volume 4.** Choose from eleven crampacked collections of classic television commercials, from random products to specialized subjects. *See* Something Weird Video for catalog info.

Crime Jazz, Music in the First Degree and *Crime Jazz, Music in the Second Degree* are among the many classic and obscure soundtrack titles and anthologies offered by Rhino Records. *See* Rhino.

Crippled Dick Hot Wax is a Berlin company with a tempting catalog of German television and film composers, exotica, Communist space operas, swingy and sophisticated soundtracks, sleazy listening, and acid jazz. A party music haven with a wonderful Web site that allows buyers to sample audio from each title of their soul-stirring collection. Reach them at www.crippled.com.

Dionysus Records specializes in hard-to-find indy labels from around the world, with a focus on garage, rockabilly, and exotica, in addition to rare vinyl. For catalog and mail order, go to www.dionysusrecords.com/mailorder/mailorder.html.

Doob Doob O'Rama, **Volume 2.** One of a two-volume set of film songs from Bollywood. Volume 2 keeps a better pace for party purposes, but both are available through Normal Records in Germany. *See* QDK Media.

Electronic Toys is one of two 1970s synthesizer music anthologies available on the Normal Records label in Germany. *See* QDK Media.

EnviroTex Lite Pour-On High Gloss Finish is usually carried in craft and hardware stores. Contact www.eti-usa.com for product information and a list of retailers.

Exquisita Decadencia. The music of Pedro Vigil is a ready-made score for any high-style social encounter. *See* Siesta Records.

The Fluid Soundbox and Lost TV Themes. *See* Dionysus Records.

Girls Come Too. One of many nudist camp classics from the vaults of Something Weird Video. *See* Something Weird Video for catalog info.

H. R. Pufnstuf Live at the Hollywood Bowl. One of many Sid and Marty Krofft titles available from Rhino Video. *See* Rhino.

Hava Narghile. *See* Dionysus Records.

Hey Folks! It's Intermission Time, Volume 5. One of six such collections offered by Something Weird Video. *See* Something Weird Video for catalog info.

I Wanna Be a Beauty Queen can be purchased at www.videoflicks.com.

Kimchi. For more information, go to www.kimchi.or.kr/english/index.html.

Kinda' Kinky is one of three top-notch party CDs from the incomparable Ursula 1000, including *The Now Sound of Ursula 1000* and *All Systems are Go-Go*. To order, reach Eighth Street Lounge Music at www.eslmusic.com.

Liberace (Boxed set). *See* Rhino.

Mixing cups for resin. For the best results, use the measured plastic mixing cup specifically created for use with ETI polyester resins. *See* Castin'Craft Polyester Resin.

Monsterama Sci-Fi Late-Night Creature Feature Show. One of countless movie trailer collections offered by the world's best source for party videos. *See* Something Weird Video.

Mystic Groove is one of many specialized world-music compilation releases on the Quango label. For information, audio samples, and ordering, reach them at www.quango.com.

A Night at the Playboy Mansion, *After the Playboy Mansion,* and the slightly more elusive *Disco Forever* are three excellent Dimitri from Paris party mixes. For information about Dimitri, go to www.respectisburning.com or www.astralwerks.com.

Nonreactive bowls. Many recipes require nonreactive cookware—pans and bowls made of or lined with materials like stainless steel, enamel, or glass—but few ever explain why this is so important. Acidic ingredients like tomatoes, lemons, limes, ginger, and even some seafoods will react with aluminum or unlined copper surfaces and take on a bitter, metallic taste. When mixing or stirring, it's also wise to stick to wooden spoons as opposed to metallic when preparing foods with acidic ingredients.

Normal Records. A treasure trove for aficionados of the obscure. The Normal catalog is impossible to categorize, ranging from Russ Meyer scores to satanic electronica. Reach them at www.qdkmedia.com.

Oceanic Arts has been the country's leading supplier of tropical decor since 1956. From coconut candleholders, seashells, and bamboo to custom-carved, fourteen-foot tiki gods, thatched umbrella covers, and tatami mats, you won't find a more all-inclusive source. Send $10 for a compete catalog to Oceanic Arts, 12414 Whittier Blvd., Whittier, CA 90602-1017, or reach them at www.oceanicarts.net.

Paris Combo. For more about Paris Combo visit www.pariscombo.com, and for ordering and information

about other Paris Combo titles visit www.amazon.com.

Plaster cloth can be ordered online through Jerry's Artarama, a comprehensive and invaluable source for a myriad of art supplies at discount prices. Reach them at www.jerryscatalog.com.

Pop-Shopping. *See* Crippled Dick Hot Wax.

Put a Flavor to Love, *Paradise Wobble,* and *Come into My Parlor* are three Janet Klein titles well worth investigation. Sample her sound and experience the odd and entrancing world of Janet Klein at www.janetklein.com

QDK Media is the parent company carrying both the QDK and Normal Records catalogs. Reach them at www.qdkmedia.com.

Rain cape thatch is sold in 3' x 4' sheets, either untreated or fire retardant. *See* Oceanic Arts.

Ramones Songbook, Nutley Brass. Visit www.themedicinelabel.com to order online.

Rhino. For music, Rhino's catalog not only provides a mouthwatering selection of R&B, doo-wop, soul, disco, latin, jazz, instrumentals, TV and film scores, novelty, and holiday titles, but also offers a wealth of information on the artists and collections. For video and DVD, the eclectic list of titles includes classic television, music videos, live concerts, music documentaries, comedy, and classic horror. Great bathroom reading. To request a catalog, visit them at www.rhino.com or www.rhinovideo.com, or call (800) 546-3670.